75

Creative Ways to
Publish Students' Writing

by

Cherlyn Sunflower

SCHOLASTIC
PROFESSIONAL BOOKS

New York • Toronto • London • Auckland • Sydney

Design by Nancy Metcalf
Production by Intergraphics
Cover design by Vincent Ceci
Cover illustrations by Helen H. Moore
Illustrations by Lynn Vinyard

ISBN 0-590-49270-5

Printed in the U.S.A.

Contents

Introduction

75 Creative Ways to Publish Students' Writing is designed for 2-6th grade teachers who want to create authentic writing experiences for their students, but need exciting ideas on ways to publish what their students write. Seven different types of publishing methods are represented.

1. Included in the book category are traditional favorites such as Hand Sewn Books, Stitched Books, Hinged Books, and Ring Books plus exciting ideas such as Pocket Books, Multiple Strip Books, and Recycled Books.

2. In the letter category your students will be excited to make Cardboard Print Cards, Folded Greeting Cards, Envelope Letters, and many others.

3. If you want students to display their compositions, you will find new favorites such as publishing on a Banner, Crown, Display Animals, Tornadoes, and Neck Tags.

4. In the special writing tools and papers category your students will love the Pads, "Leather Hides", Adding Machine Tape, and many more from which to choose.

5. Included in the code category are old favorites such as Secret Crayon Messages, Pencil Wrap Codes, and others.

6. Then in the miscellaneous category are interesting publishing methods such as Flip'em Charts, Certificates, Kitchen Magnets, and many more.

These ideas will compliment your writing program by offering 75 exciting ways students can publish in the 1990s.

These publishing ideas use inexpensive or easy-to-get materials and require only common classroom tools. Our easy to follow directions are clear and contain plenty of step by step illustrations. Another advantage is that your students do the "work". However, both you and your students will, we hope, have lots of fun.

Getting Started

Students who value writing as a form of communication write because they have a desire to say something. As you plan an authentic writing experience keep in mind that your students need two things: a real purpose for communicating and a real audience. Without these elements, writing or going through the steps of the writing process can become a boring and meaningless task. *75 Creative Ways to Publish Students' Writing* adds a bit of magic to the experience and helps students feel their ideas and feelings are valued.

1. Establish a significant purpose for communicating. Six common purposes include:

- to convey information or thoughts: a warning, a campaign flyer, a for-sale notice, a recipe, travel directions, a movie review, a survival manual, and a reward poster.

- to share feelings and/or opinions: a sympathy card, an apology note, a cheer, a valentine message, congratulations, a thank you note, and a letter of complaint.

- to request something: a Dear Santa letter, a poll or survey, a get well card, an advertisement, an application letter, an excuse, a plea, and a petition.

- to extend memory: an IOU, a things to do list, a remember to pack note, a contract, a travel log, a calender, and a log of science observations.

- to clarify feelings: a diary entry, an autobiography or memoirs.

- to organize thoughts: a grocery list, a budget, a schedule, a wish list, and a learning log.

- to entertain others: an adventure story, riddles, jokes, a word search, a tongue twister, and a song.

You'll find publishing methods included in this book appropriate for each of these purposes.

2. Then you or your students need to think about who will be their audience. As you think of an audience consider some of these options:

- parents or another trusted adult.

- peers, friends, older and younger children.

- people in the community, local businesses, a sports hero, actors.

- politicians, people in the news.

- unknown audiences such as the local paper, newsletter, magazine.

- self.

To become skilled communicators your students need multiple daily communication opportunities and many kinds of real audiences to respond to their compositions, not just teacher as evaluator.

You'll find appropriate methods included in this book for all different kinds of audiences.

3. After that you or your students need to think about many different types of writing that help organize ideas, such as:

- narrative writings,

- descriptive writings,

- persuasive writings,

- "how to" writings,

- songs, and

- poetry.

You'll find publishing methods included here for each of these different types of writing.

4. Now guide your students through the writing process.

5. Once students have written their compositions it is time to share how they will be presented. You will find your students' motivation is affected by what happens to their compositions. If writings will only be collected then posted or graded then discarded, students often will not see that you value their work. By involving your students in authentic communication situations, you will teach them to value writing as an important communication tool and to be sensitive to situations in which a written response is needed. Daily writing opportunities with varied audiences and purposes are necessary to develop communication skills.

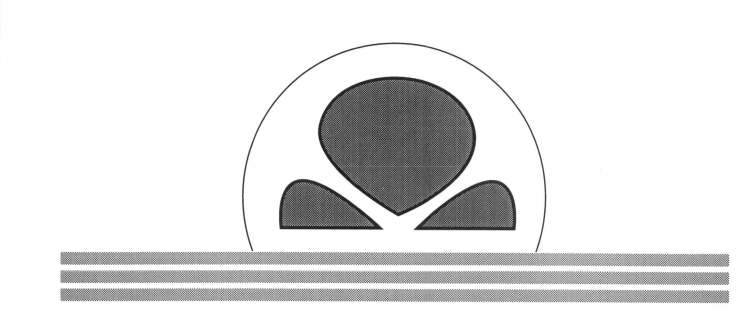

Books

Accordion Books

The Broken Bike
A True Story

Materials:

- craft paper or lightweight oaktag cut into 3" x 5" rectangles • rough draft writing paper
- scissors • hole punch • fine line markers • ribbon or yarn cut to pieces 15" long.

Directions:

1. Fold entire length of paper in half.

2. Use hole punch to punch hole close to fold.

3. Fold in half again.

4. Fold each double layered end of paper up to center to form a "W" shape.

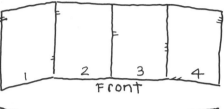

5. Have students use separate paper to write and illustrate stories consisting of one beginning part, two middle parts and one ending part.

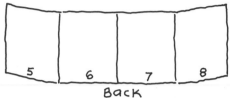

6. Ask students to number the pages of the books 1-8.

7. Have students transfer polished story segments and illustrations (in an alternating writing/illustration/writing/illustration pattern) to pages of the accordion books.

8. Fold books closed. Thread yarn or ribbon through hole, and tie around books to hold shut.

OTHER

Possibilities for Your Students

- After you fold all the pages, lay a simple shape such as a pumpkin over the front cover. Trace around the shape. Next cut out the shape as you would paper dolls. Finally use felt tip pens or felt to decorate the cover of your Accordion Book.

- Glue a cardboard cover to the front and back of each Accordion Book to make it stronger.

- Make an accordion book out of tag board so that it will stand up. Cut out pages one at a time and tape the pages together.

- Glue a head on the front of the book and a tail to the last page.

Coupon Books

This Coupon is good for
letting you ride my bike
to the park
Expiration Date: 2/9/95

≡ Materials:

• copies of the coupons "kit" printed on pages 14 and 15 • scissors • pencils • crayons •
decorative craft supplies (colored glue, glitter, stickers, etc.)

≡ Directions:

1. Offer each student a copy of the coupon "kit" on pages 14 and 15.

2. Have students cut apart coupon covers and coupon.

3. Invite students to use the coupons to grant recipients a special wish or service.

4. Invite students to add color and decorations (stickers, spot art, glued-on glitter, etc.) to
each coupon.

OTHER
Possibilities for Your Students

• Have students design their own coupons, or try
making shaped coupon books for many
occasions: birthdays, Valentine's Day, You Look
Like You Need a Helper, and Get Well Soon.

• Create Gift Certificates instead of coupons.

This coupon good for: letting you borrow my sweater from Laisha

Gift Certificate for One funny Joke or help with the dishes
Expiration Date 9/29/95

This Coupon is good for

_____

_____

EXPIRATION DATE _____

This Coupon is good for

_____

_____

EXPIRATION DATE _____

This Coupon is good for

_____

_____

EXPIRATION DATE _____

Coupon
Book

To: _____ From: _____

This Coupon is good for

_____ _____

_____ _____

EXPIRATION DATE: _____

This Coupon is good for

_____

_____

EXPIRATION DATE _____

Fan Paged Books

Materials:

• writing paper, approximately 8 1/2" x 11" • ruler • paper cutter • stapler

Directions:

1. Decide on the number of fan-page books you are going to assemble.

2. Decide on the number of pages in each fan-page book.

3. To make a pattern for each page of the book's pages, hold the paper horizontally and use a ruler to mark off 1" wide increments from the right hand margin of the paper.

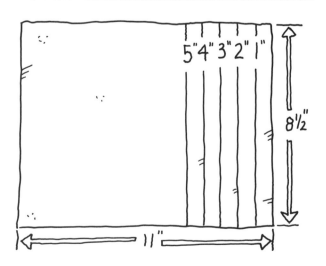

4. Place this marked paper over another piece of paper and use paper cutter to trim off the first 1" segment.

5. Repeat, trimming away one more inch from each new piece of paper, until you have prepared the number of descending-size pages you wish to have for each book.

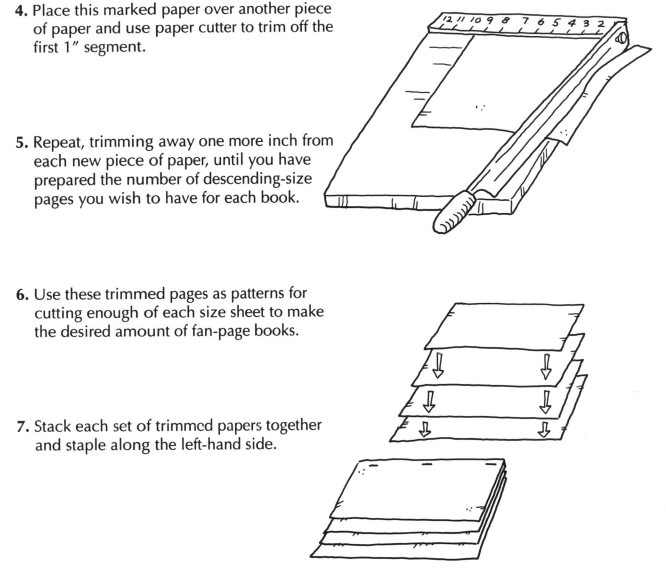

6. Use these trimmed pages as patterns for cutting enough of each size sheet to make the desired amount of fan-page books.

7. Stack each set of trimmed papers together and staple along the left-hand side.

OTHER
Possibilities for Your Students

- Use different colored paper for each page of your book.
- Have students use the books for autograph books or as mini-photo albums.

Hand-Sewn Books

Materials:

• wallpaper scraps (trimmed to pieces 8 1/2" x 11") • copy paper • large plastic craft needles • sharp metal craft needle • yarn • paper clips • marker

Directions:

1. Fold wallpaper in half right-side-out and crease with finger nail.

2. Stack desired number of copy papers together, fold in half and crease.

3. Place folded papers inside folded wallpaper cover.

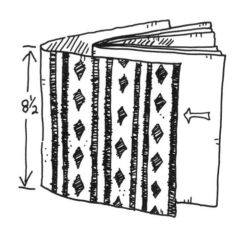

4. Using paper clips, clip cover to pages.

5. Open unbound book to center.

6. Using marker, print a series of dots down the center crease of the paper spread.

7. Use a metal needle to pierce the dots through to the paper cover, thus creating "guide holes."

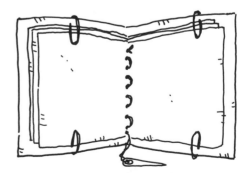

8. Have students use yarn and plastic needles to bind the pages and cover together by sewing through the guide holes.

Hinged Books

Materials:

• cardboard • construction paper • writing paper • paper fasteners • 2-3 inch wide plastic or masking tape • glue • scissors • hole punch

Directions:

1. Cut two pieces of cardboard 8 inches by 12 inches or slightly larger than the pages to be published.

2. Cut construction paper the same size as the cardboard covers. Then glue the contruction paper to one side of each (cardboard) cover.

3. Cut a one inch strip from the left hand side of the front cover. This will allow the book to fold open. Don't cut the back cover.

4. Next lay the two parts of the front cover beside each other. Leave a 1/4 inch gap between the two front cover pieces.

5. Use wide plastic or masking tape to connect the 1 inch strip to the front cover. When you do this, be sure to leave a 1/4 inch gap between the two pieces. If you forget to leave enough space, your Hinged Book won't open correctly.

6. (Optional) Glue a small rectangle with the title and author's name to the front cover.

7. Punch three holes in the front and back covers.

8. Next, put the front cover over the pages to be published. Punch three matching holes in these lined pages.

9. Now assemble the front cover, lined pages, and back cover and insert a paper fastener through each hole.

10. Finally, fold the front cover back and crease the fold.

Pocket Books

Materials:

• envelopes saved from greeting cards, discarded stationary or junk mail • 8 1/2" x 11" paper stapled together to create booklet • glue

Directions:

1. At the bottom of each right-hand page in each booklet, glue one envelope, flap-side-up.

2. In the space above each envelope, print a riddle or question.

3. Print the answer to the riddle or question on a small card and slip card into the envelope.

4. Have students use the left-hand side of each page to provide an illustration corresponding to the question, the riddle or the answer.

Possibilities for Your Students

- Ask parents to collect colorful envelopes that they receive. Even though a name and/or an address is written on the front of the envelope, the envelopes can be used because only the open side of the envelope will be used.

face side down

- Nursing homes and retirement communities receive many cards with colorful envelopes. Most directors and seniors will be glad to assist your elementary school.

- Instead of using envelopes make your own out of construction paper. Fold any sized paper in half and staple the two ends together. Leave the top open or make envelopes with a folded flap.

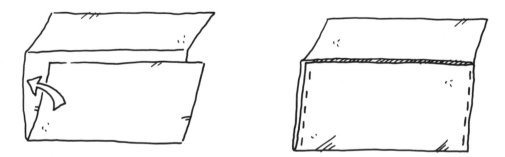

- Share the Pocket Books *The Jolly Postman* by Janet and Allan Ahlberg and/or *Jolly Christmas Postman* by Janet and Allan Ahlberg (Little Brown, 1986 and 1991).

- Jokes can also be shared via pocket books. Have students write jokes at the top of each page and punch lines on slips of paper tucked into pockets.

Dear _____ ,

Your friend,

_____

Recycled Books

Materials:

- reusable materials featuring attractive photos or illustrations, such as: outdated spiral-bound wall calendars, photo-journal magazines and discarded picture books
- construction paper • scissors • glue

Directions:

1. Glue construction paper directly over any printed text.

2. Trim to size.

3. Have students write their own text to accompany pictures.

OTHER
Possibilities for Your Students

- Clip interesting photos or illustrations from discarded calendars, books and magazines. Glue these to construction paper and use to create a photo file to dislodge writer's block.

- Cover the text only on discarded children's picture books. Have students write new text to accompany pictures.

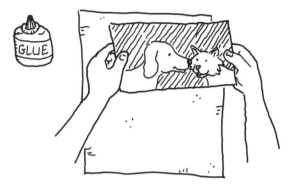

- Use class discussion to demonstrate how asking who, what, when, where and why questions about the pictures can pique curiosities and offer inspirations to write.

Ring Books

Materials:

• metal loose leaf rings or metal shower curtain pins • hole puncher • unlined index cards (larger size cards for younger students; smaller size cards for older students)
• markers and crayons

Directions:

1. Punch one hole along edge of each card as shown.

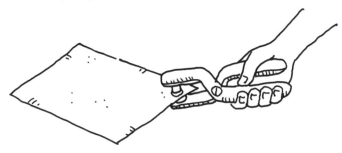

2. Insert rings or pins through holes in cards; lock rings or pins shut.

3. Have students use one side of each card to record storylines or sentences.

4. Then, have students use the other side of the cards to illustrate their text.

Possibilities for Your Students

- Have younger students dictate a word-a-day that they would like to learn to recognize. Record each word on one side of an index card, then have students use the other side of the card to illustrate each word. Students use rings to bind their accumulated their sight-word files. Files may be hung from hooks inserted into pegboard, or displayed standing along the edge of a chalkboard, or in stands cut from discarded file folders. (Hint: to make stands, place copies of the pattern on page 28 on top of file folders matching folded edges, to pattern as shown. Trace, cut and open.)

- Ring Books can also be made by punching the holes in the top left corner or by punching a hole in both the top left and top right corners of each index card.

- Long thin Ring Books can be make from colored construction paper and yarn. Laminating each piece of construction paper will make it more durable.

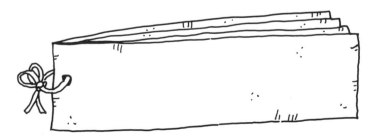

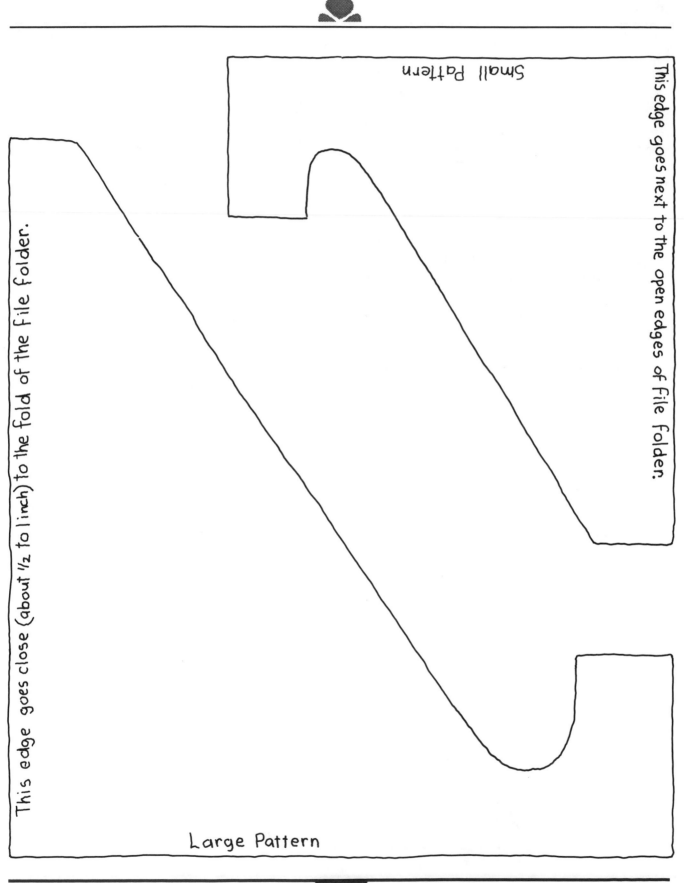

This edge goes next to the open edges of File Folder.

Small Pattern

This edge goes close (about 1/2 to 1 inch) to the fold of the File Folder.

Large Pattern

Sequence Books

Materials:

• construction paper • ruler • pencil • glue • scissors • copy paper • lined writing paper (for older students only)

Directions:

1. Fold construction paper in half lengthwise.

2. Decide on the number of equal segments (two, three, four...) you wish your book to have, then use ruler to measure and mark off your paper accordingly.

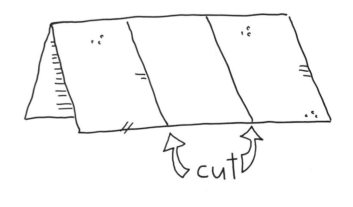

3. Cut along lines to fold, thus creating flaps.

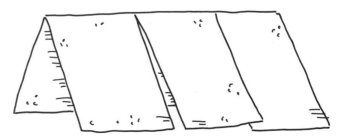

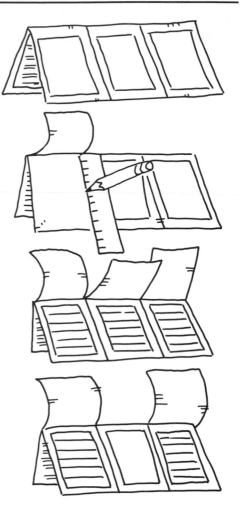

4. On top of closed flaps, glue sequence pictures, or fold copy paper in half lengthwise, and cut into the same number of equal segments as you created with the construction paper. Glue one picture or one section of copy paper to each flap.

5. Lift each flap and use ruler to create lines on inside of the book corresponding to edges of flaps.

6. Cut copy paper (or writing paper) into segments slightly smaller than those created by lines on the construction paper. Glue one segment of copy or writing paper into each of the construction paper spaces.

7. Have students write stories (thoughts, reflections...) on the inside segments of the books and then illustrate their words on the corresponding outside flaps (or vice-versa!).

(Note: Sequencing skills are developmentally based. Emerging writers who are just beginning to recognize sequence of events in pictures or a storyline, may not be ready to create sequential stories unassisted. Instead, it may be enough for them to write or dictate an idea on the inside of the book and then provide a corresponding illustration on the covering flap, without needing to relate the pictures and writings in a left-to-right sequence.)

OTHER Possibilities for Your Students

- Experiment with Sequence Books with two, four, or more flaps.

- Switch the location of the pictures and the lined paper. The pictures could be on the inside and the story on the outside.

Shape Books

≡ Materials:

• construction paper • copy or lined writing paper • precut stencils or tracing shapes (pages 32, 33, and 34, or use students' artwork as the basis for shapes) scissors • stapler

≡ Directions:

1. Provide older students with supplies listed above.

2. Have each student select a stencil to trace and cut out corresponding shapes from two pieces of construction paper (for covers) and as many pages as needed from copy or writing paper.

3. Or, have each student draw a favorite shape on manila paper, cut the shape out and use to create a matching back cover and inside book pages as described above.

4. Stack and staple shape books together along left-hand edge.

5. To avoid waste, have all students work their rough draft ideas through on scrap paper before transferring their polished pieces to the shape books.

OTHER
Possibilities for Your Students

• Allow younger students to each select or design a shape for you to precut and preassemble into a book.

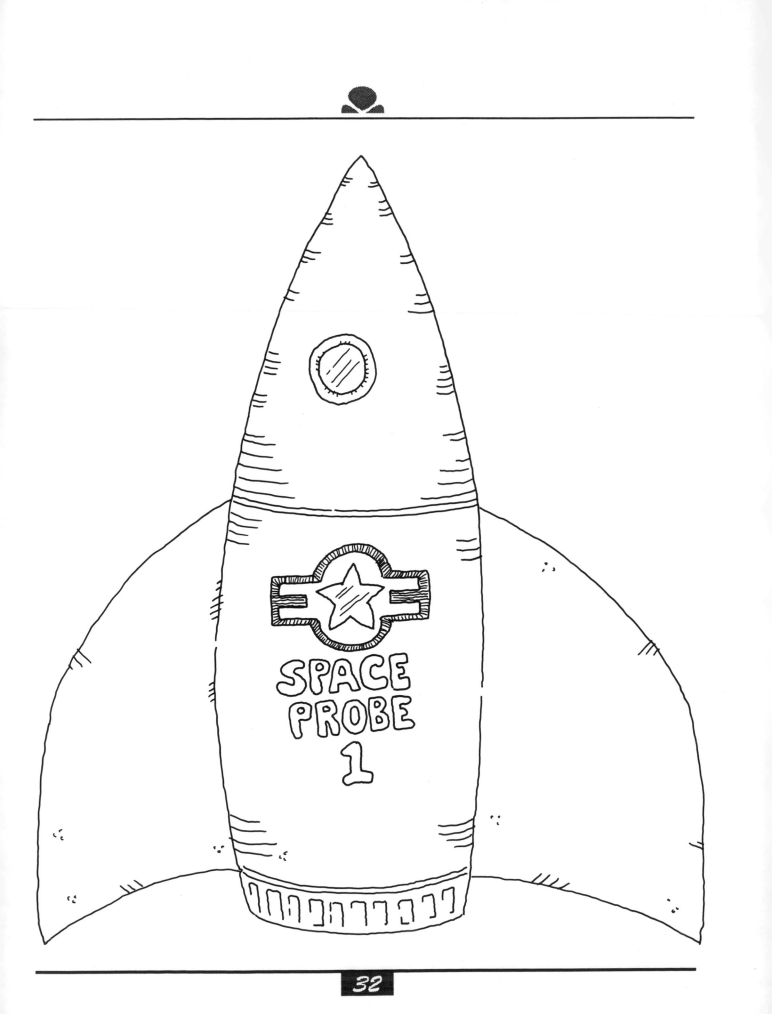

Stitched Books

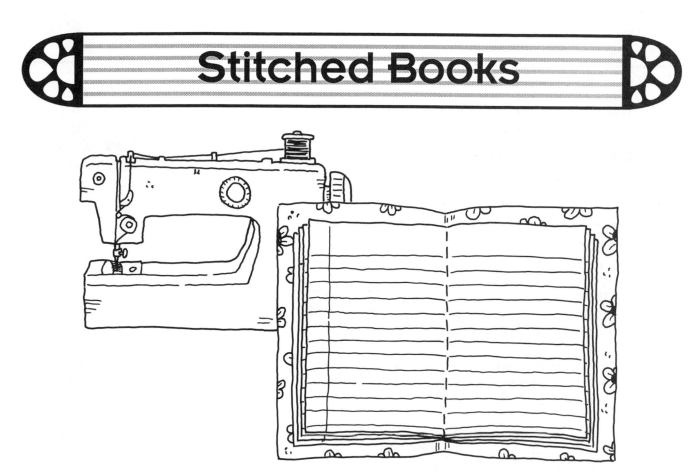

Materials:

- sewing machine • thread • scissors • fabric glue • copy paper or lined writing paper
- remnants from heavyweight fabric (denim, felt, wool, etc.) • lightweight cardboard (cereal boxes work well)

Directions (to make one book):

1. Cut two pieces of cardboard (7" x 5 1/2").

2. Cut two pieces of fabric (8 1/2" x 12 1/2").

3. Squeeze a thin line of glue along the edge of one side of each piece of cardboard.

4. Place cardboard pieces, glue-side-down, on the wrong side of the fabric so that there is a 1/2" space between cardboard pieces, and a fabric margin of 1/2" to 3/4" extending around edge of cardboard.

Fabric-Face Down

5. Squeeze a thin line of glue along the edge of the exposed side of each piece of cardboard.

6. Place remaining fabric piece right-side-up over first fabric piece, sandwiching cardboard pieces inside and aligning fabric edges and corners.

7. Cut a supply of of 8 1/2" x 11" copy or lined writing paper in half horizontally thus forming paper segments equaling 8 1/2" x 5 1/2".

8. Stack three, four or five of these paper segments together and, holding paper horizontally, fold left side to right. Crease.

9. Place creased paper into book spine space located between two fabric-covered cardboard segments of book. Secure in place with paper clips.

10. Sew pages to cover using long basting stitch. Clip and tie ends of thread off.

11. If desired, use zig-zag stitch to bind raw edges of book closed.

12. Invite students to use books for journal or diary writings. (Hint: These books make great gifts to give to students!)

OTHER Possibilities for Your Students

- On the first page of the Stitched Book, add the name of the publishing company such as "Ms. Young's 4th Grade," place of publication, copyright date.

- Use a zig-zag stitch all the way around the cloth margins to keep the cloth from fraying.

Materials:

- sewing machine • discarded wallpaper sample book or remnants from heavyweight fabric (denim, felt, wool, etc.) • thread • copy or lined writing paper • scissors

Directions:

1. Trim wallpaper samples or fabric remnants into 9" x11" rectangles.

2. Stack desired number of copy or lined writing papers between book covers. Pin covers and pages together.

3. Set sewing machine to zig-zag setting and sew along left-hand edge of each book, allowing for 3/8" margin. Clip and tie ends of thread off.

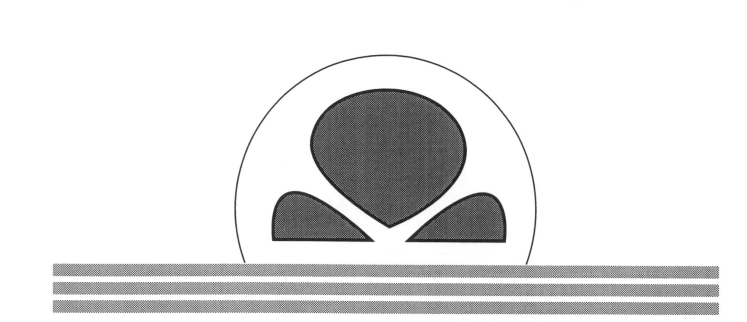

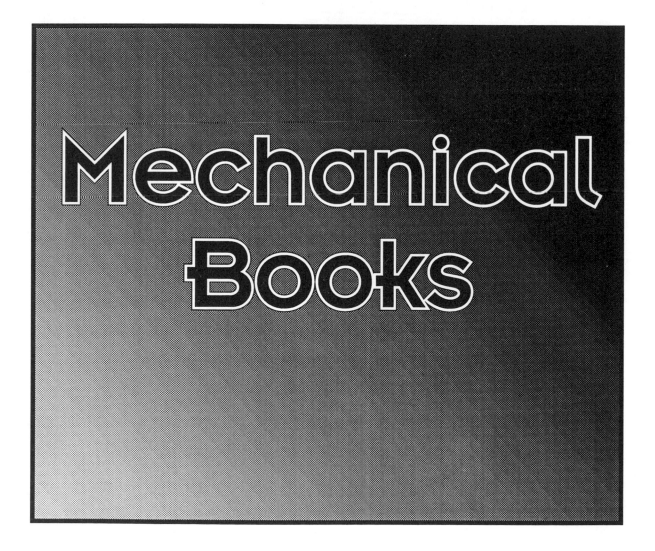

Mechanical Books

Pop-Out Personalities

Title _____

by _____

_____

_____

_____

☰ Materials:

• copies of folded mouth illustration on page 42 • scissors • copies of writing paper on page 43.

☰ Directions:

1. Make copies of page 42 and cut in half as indicated.

2. Offer students each one copy of the folded mouth illustration.

3. Instruct students to fold and crease their papers in half so that mouth lines are on either side of folds.

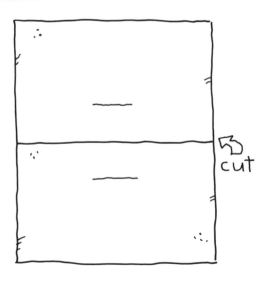

4. Have students clip open mouth lines and then fold top and bottom halves of mouths to one side, thus forming triangle shapes.

5. After creasing along folds, have students fold and crease triangle shapes to other side of paper.

6. Have students open paper flat, turn paper over and refold paper inside out along center crease.

7. Then, have students refold and re-crease triangle shapes to front and back of folded paper.

8. Students may then open paper up, push top and bottom of each mouth forward and glue paper (all except mouth piece) to top of writing paper (pg. 43).

9. Have students use markers to add details to face, and to use space below for writing.

OTHER
Possibilities for Your Students

- Suggest that students add details so that completed pop-out personalities resemble real or fictitious characters. Students may then write about the characters in space beneath their pop-out personalities.)

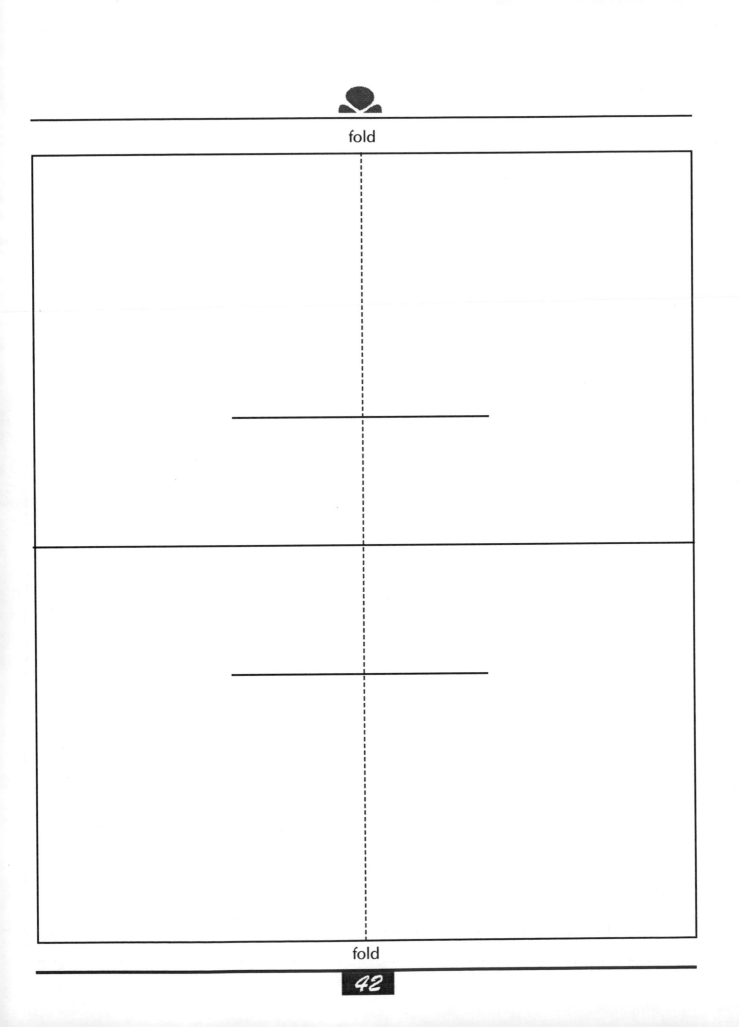

fold

fold

Title _____

by _____

_____

_____

_____

_____

_____

_____

_____

_____

Pop-Up Books

Materials:

• copies of pages 46 and 47 • scissors • construction paper • photographs, stickers, pictures cut from greeting cards, small illustrations (approximately 3"x3") created on pieces cut from discarded manila file folders • glue

Directions:

1. Provide each student with several copies of page 46.

2. Instruct each student to fold paper in half and clip to dots along two lines indicated to create pop-up tab.

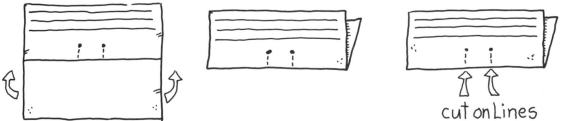

cut on Lines

3. Have each student open the paper up, gently slip an index finger behind either side of pop-up tab and pull forward in order to crease on line labeled "Fold."

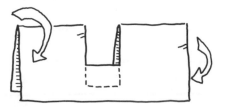

4. Then, while continuing to pinch the fold of the pop-up tab together, each student should turn paper over and make creases at both bases of tab (located between the two sets of dots) thus allowing pop-up tab to be folded between the two halves of the paper.

5. After opening papers up, students may glue pictures to the front of the pop-up tabs. (When glued in place, pictures should not cover the bottom fold of the pop-up tab or page will not close properly.)

6. Foreground of paper may serve as area for students to record writings.

7. Students may illustrate background as desired.

8. Repeat above process for each page of book. When ready to bind pages together, fold each page shut and stack together in proper sequence. Then, glue the bottom half of one sheet to the top half of the next sheet.

9. Pages may be glued inside a folded construction paper cover, or use copies of cover on page 47.

OTHER
Possibilities for Your Students

- Cut tabs for more than one pop-up picture per page. Or, make different sized pop-ups appear at different dimensions on one page by varying the depth of the cuts for each tab created.

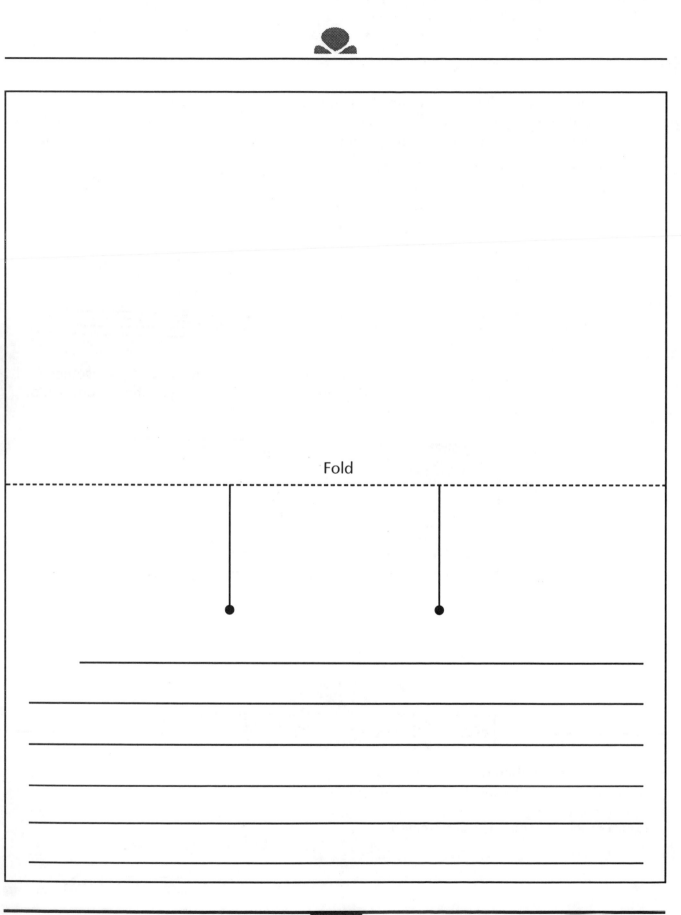

Fold

My Pop-Up Book

by

Springy Pop-Outs

Moon
Craters, lifeless
Rotating, moving
turning
Asteroid

Materials:

• construction paper • scissors • glue • tape • pictures (cut from magazines, wrapping paper or greeting cards) or characters or objects cut from original illustrations
• construction paper strips 1/2 " wide x 7" long (two strips per illustration)

Directions:

1. Have students draw or cut out a number of illustrations or pictures to accompany a piece of writing. Pictures or illustrations may be of any size, but must be smaller than the pages used to create book.

2. Use white glue to mount pictures or illustrations on construction paper and trim construction paper to size of picture or illustration.

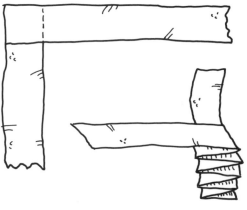

3. Position one end of each of two strips together to form "L" shaped strips

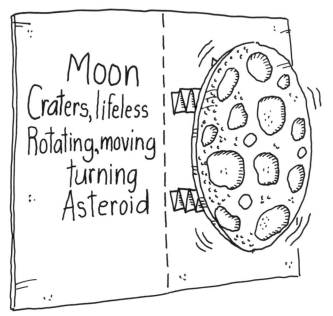

4. Glue or tape two ends of strips together, and let dry if necessary.

5. Have students begin folding one strip over other at point of conjuncture. Then, have them fold second strip over first. Have students continue folding to ends of strips.

6. Instruct students to glue one end of each spring to the back of an illustration or picture of their choice, and the other to a page of a book they are constructing. As pages are turned, illustration will now appear to spring out at the reader.

7. If desired, students may add background details (before or after gluing process) to page to enhance springy pop-out effect.

Possibilities for Your Students

• If an illustration is oversize, students may need to glue two or more springs to picture's back.

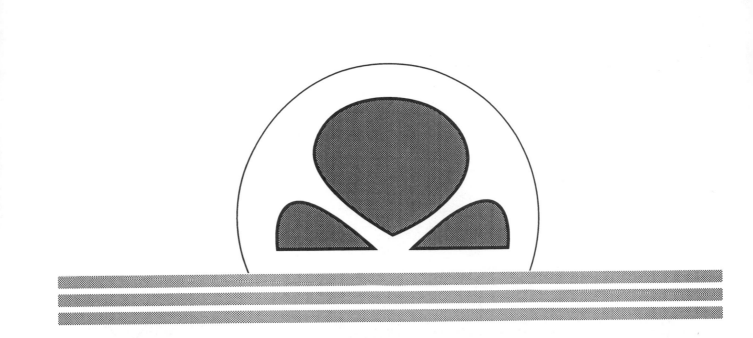

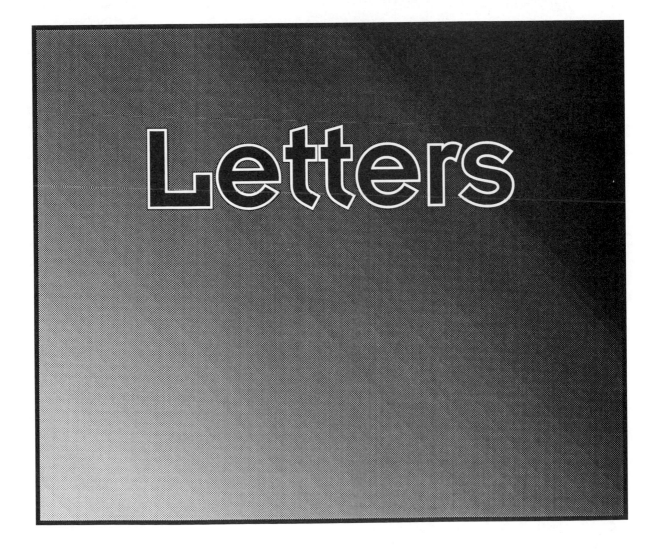

Letters

Cardboard Rubbing Cards

Materials:

- copies of page 54 • cardboard, oaktag or discarded file folders • scissors • glue
- crayons or colored pencils • pencils

Directions:

1. Offer each student a copy of the card on page 54. have students fold papers in half so that lines appear on inside of fold. Set aside.

2. Then, have students use pencils and cardboard to draw or cut shapes of their own design (or provide students with a supply of shapes to trace). Younger students may need to have cardboard shapes precut for them.

3. Instruct students to glue cardboard shapes to 1/2 sheet of copy paper (previously used paper is perfect for gluing shapes on to).

4. After letting shapes dry, have students slip sheets with shapes inside folded cards.

5. Students then rub the sides of crayons without wrappers or the side tips of colored pencils over folded card. Rubbings representing glued-down shapes will appear on card.

6. After removing shapes, students may write messages on outside and inside of cards.

Possibilities for Your Students

• Glue rickrack on the lower edge under your message.

Fold

Materials:

- large detergent box with hinged lid • craft knife (adult use only) • blue craft paper
- scissors • glue or tape • markers

Directions:

1. Cover box with craft paper.

2. Use red marker to label container "CLASS MAIL."

3. Use craft knife to cut slot in container lid.

4. Place mailbox in your writing corner along with a supply of envelopes (saved from junk mail) and a sign announcing times of pick-up and delivery. (Hint: Develop these times with your class.)

5. Invite students to use the envelopes provided to send each other messages through the class mail system. Have students volunteers take turns delivering mail to the rest of the class.

OTHER
Possibilities for Your Students

• To provide individual mailboxes for receiving mail, have each student cover a coffee can or shoe box and then label with his or her name.

Envelope Letters

Materials:

- copies of the fold-over note on page 58 • scissors • pencils, crayons or markers • glue
- postage stamps (optional)

Directions:

1. Provide each student with one or more copies of the fold-over note on page 58.

2. Instruct students to cut the notes out along the heavy lines, being careful not to cut on the dotted "fold" lines.

3. Have students flip notes over and use reverse side of the paper to draw a picture and/or write a message to a friend or family member. Students should avoid writing on the note flaps as these will be glued down to create the envelope.

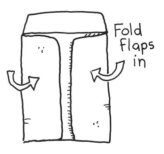

4. After students have completed their message, have them flip the note back over again and fold closed along the line indicated.

5. Have students apply a small amount of glue to the note flaps and glue in place.

6. When glue dries, help children complete the address and return address portion of the envelope. If desired, notes may be stamped for regular mail delivery, or delivered in person to the lucky recipient.

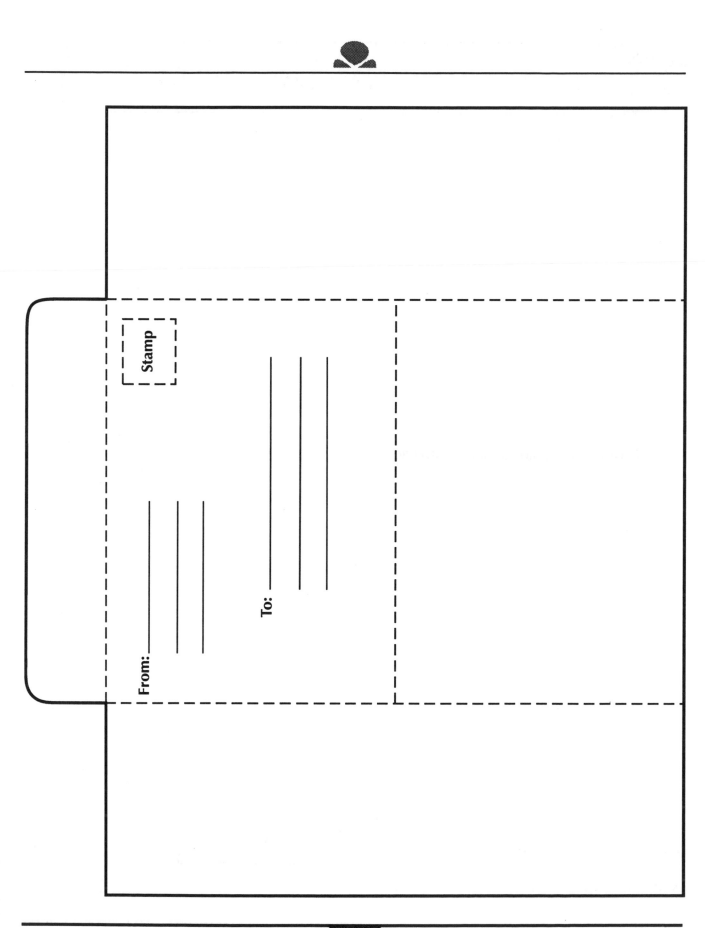

Stamp

From:

To:

Finger Print Stationery

Materials:

• new sponges • tempera paints • brush • water • pencil • copy paper • envelopes (ask parents to provide greeting card and stationery leftovers) • fine-tipped markers

Directions:

1. Wet sponges and wring almost dry.

2. Brush one color of paint onto each sponge. (Thin paint with water, if necessary.)

3. Provide small groups of students with paper, envelopes and sponge "ink pads."

4. Working in small groups (in order to share paint-coated sponges), have students press fingertips and thumbs into paint and then onto papers and envelopes to create finger and thumb prints.

5. After prints have dried, provide students with markers and invite them to add details (eyes, noses, tails, ears, hair, limbs) to their prints.

6. Have students try adding prints to greeting cards, postcards, fold-over notes, etc.

OTHER
Possibilities for Your Students

•Washable ink pads may be used instead of paint-coated sponges.

Folded Greeting Cards

Materials:

- copy paper or manila paper - markers and crayons - pencils

Directions:

1. Have students fold paper in half and in half again.

2. Encourage students to begin written message on the front of card, completing message on inside of card. (Hint: For inspiration provide students with an assortment of commercially prepared cards.)

3. Students may then add illustrations to complete cards. Front of cards may also be decorated with yarn, glued-on glitter or glued-on googlie eyes.

4. Provide students with envelopes to accommodate cards. (Visit your local greeting card store and ask proprietor to save you any unused envelopes from greeting cards.)

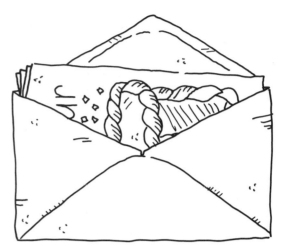

Possibilities for Your Students

• Make copies of card covers on page 62 and 63. Two examples are attached but you can create your own illustrations.

• Create covers by gluing on rick-rack to one edge and adding dried flowers or other objects to the cover.

• Cards can be made for many purposes: Thank You Notes, Friendly Letters, Sympathy Cards, Invitations, etc.

Letters to Public Officials

Materials:

- paper • stamped envelopes • pencils, pens or markers

Directions:

1. Help students decide on individual issues they wish to address.

2. Discover (through a series of phone calls to local officials) which public official is responsible for affecting each issue.

3. Help students draft letters explaining their concerns, viewpoints and suggestions to the official of their choice. Show students proper business letter form. (Modern format directs us to align each of the five parts of the letter [return address and date, inside address, greeting, body, closure and signature] along the left-hand margin without paragraph indentations.

4. Help students address envelopes as shown below.

5. Share letters before mailing and keep track of responses students receive from officials.

Addresses and Greetings for Public Officials

United States Representatives

President
The President
The White House
Washington, DC 20500
Dear Mr. or Ms. President:

Senator (U.S.)
The Honorable_____,
United States Senate
Washington, DC 20510
Dear Senator:

Congress (U.S.)
The Honorable_____,
House of Representatives
Washington, DC 20515
Dear Congressman or Congesswoman

State Representatives

Governor
The Honorable_____,
Governor
Capital City, State, Zip Code
Dear Governor:

Senator (State)
The Honorable _____,
State Office Building or State Capital
Capital City, State, Zip Code
Dear Senator:

Representative (State)
The Honorable_____,
State Office Building
Capitol City, State, Zip Code
Dear Congressman or
Congresswoman:

Mail Pouches

Materials:

- paper plates • yarn cut into 3' long pieces • masking tape • scissors • hole punch
- paper clips • markers • stickers (optional)

Directions:

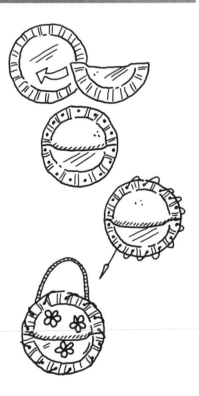

1. For each pouch, you will need one whole paper plate and one plate which has been cut in half.

2. Place half plate on top of whole plate so that rounded edges are aligned; use paper clips to hold top and bottom plate pieces together.

3. Use paper punch to punch evenly spaced holes around edge of plates.

4. Knot one end of each piece of yarn. Then, wrap masking tape around the other end so yarn doesn't fray as students work.

5. Invite students to use overhand stitch to sew around entire pouch edge, knotting end of yarn when through.

6. Demonstrate how extra yarn may be used to create handle for pouch.

7. Have students label pouches with their names. Students may then use markers and stickers to decorate pouches.

8. Pouches may be tied or taped to sides of students' desks or tacked to a bulletin board.

9 Students may then use pouches to deliver and receive written messages.

Post Cards

Materials:

- used greeting cards • index cards • glue • scissors • ruler

Directions:

1. Open greeting card along fold. Cut back off greeting card and discard.

2. Turn greeting card front over and glue to index card so that any print on inside of card will be covered. Trim excess card away so that index card fits within greeting card cover. (This entire step is unnecessary if underside of greeting card is blank.)

3. Hold card face down and horizontally. Then, use a ruler to draw a vertical line down the middle of the card, creating spaces for an address and postcard greeting.

Glue Greeting card to Index card

4. Show students where to place messages, addresses and stamps (if placing in real mail) to postcards.

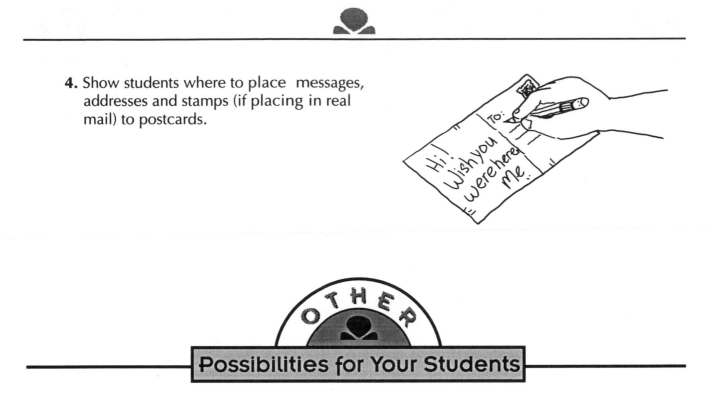

OTHER
Possibilities for Your Students

- Leave greeting cards intact and cover any writing with glued-down index cards. Encourage students to create new messages for the old cards.)

≡Materials:

- copies of the note papers on page 70 (copied on to recycled or used paper, if possible)
- markers and crayons • stapler • shoe box or small plastic baskets

≡Directions:

1. Cut apart the note papers featured on page 70.

2. Place these into a box or sort into baskets (or staple together to make mini-memo pads).

3. Place note papers in writing corner for students to use.

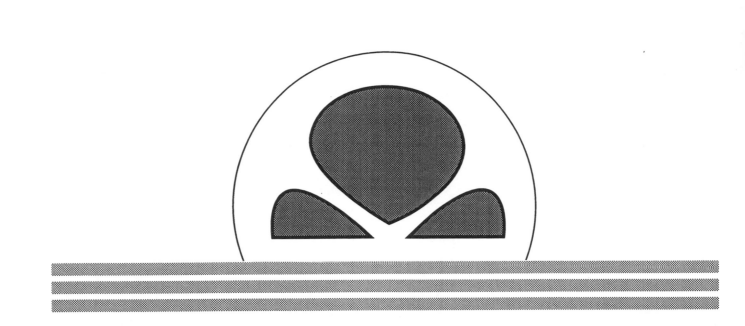

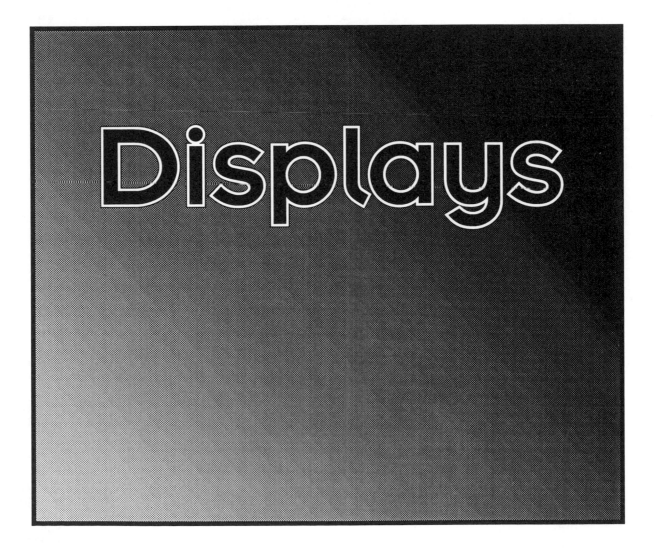

Displays

Balloon Racers

ENDOFSCHOOL PARTY
When: May 24th at 2:1?
Where: School Cafeteria
What: Refreshments and Kickball

≡ Materials:

• oaktag or cardboard (backs of used tablets or empty cereal boxes that have been flattened and opened out work well.) • copies of shoe patterns from pages 74 through 77 • 8" or 10" balloons • glue, scissors • medium tip ball point pens • colored markers or crayons

≡ Directions:

1. Have students each color a pair of "shoes" with crayons or colored markers.

2. Instruct students to cut out around the "shoes". Be sure to keep the "shoes" as one piece.

3. Now glue the shoes to the tagboard or cardboard to make them stronger.

4. When the glue is dried, cut the cardboard around the shoes.

5. Next, use your scissors to punch a small hole in the small center circle between the shoes. Be careful to keep the hole small. If the hole is too large, the balloon will not stay attached to its shoes.

6. Blow up the balloons for the students. Each balloon needs to be firm enough to write on, but not so taut that it will pop when you write on it.

7. Tie a knot at the end of the balloon.

8. Have students write messages on balloons with ball point pens.

9. Finally, pull the knotted end of each balloon through a hole in a pair of shoes until the balloon stands straight

10. Tape the knotted end of the balloon flat to the bottom side of the shoes. The shoes will serve as a base for the balloon.

Possibilities for Your Students

- Many banks, fast food places, grocery stores, and hardware stores will give teachers balloons. Call your local chamber of commerce for assistance. Larger, light colored balloons work the best. Advertisement on one side is fine.
- Create a face base in place of the shoe base. The balloon then becomes the nose on the face.

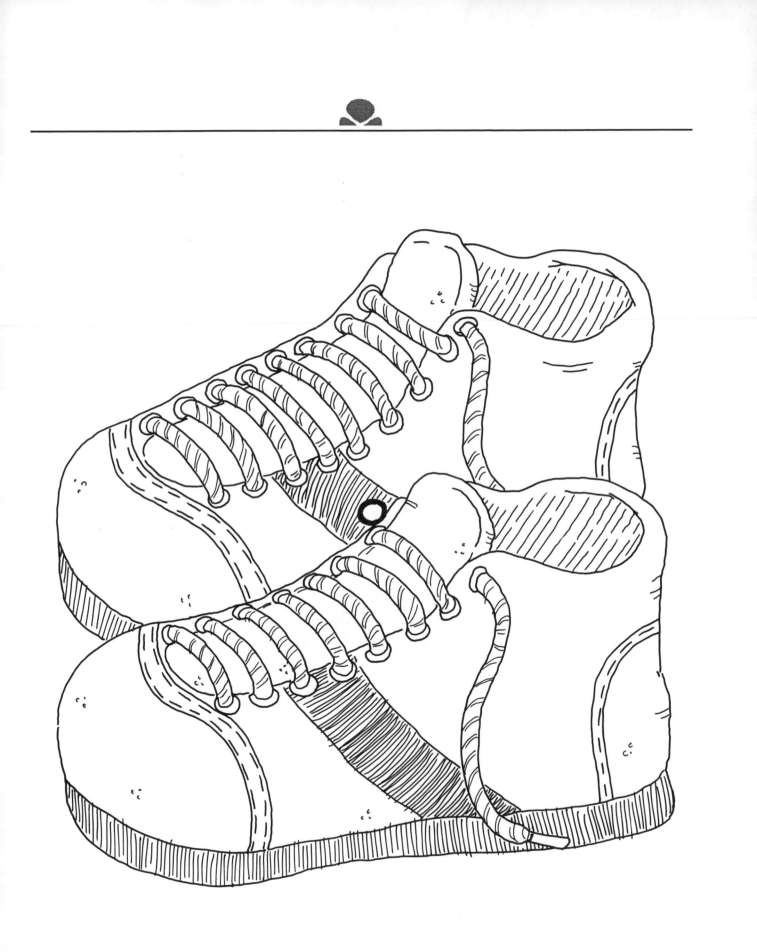

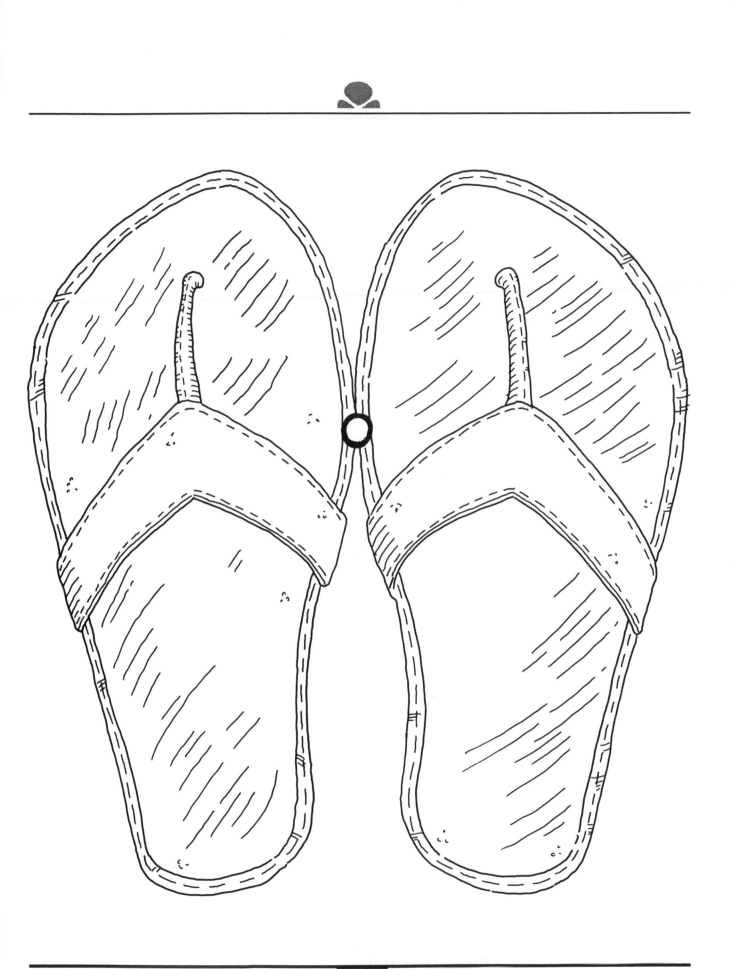

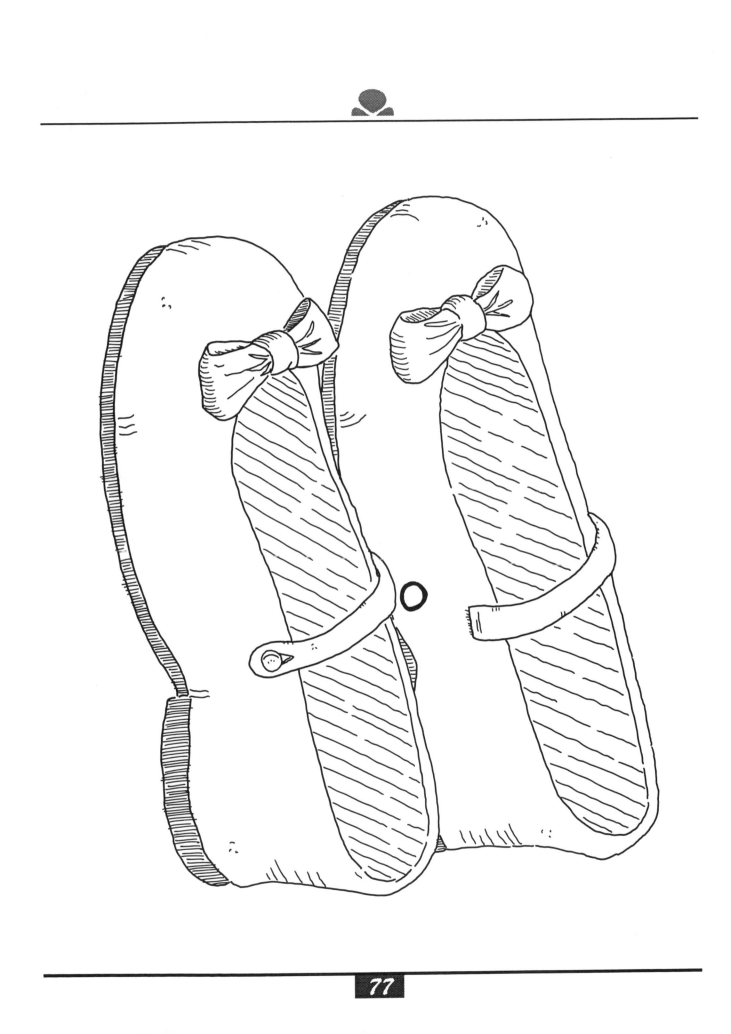

Banners

≡ Materials:

- craft or butcher paper • yarn cut into 3' long pieces • scissors • stapler • glue • crayons
- markers

≡ Directions:

1. Cut paper into banners (approximately 12" wide x 36" long), dovetailing one banner with another as you cut.

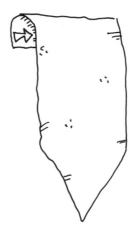

2. Trim top off each banner and fold over creating a two inch flap.

3. Cut a 3' piece of yarn and knot ends of each piece of yarn together.

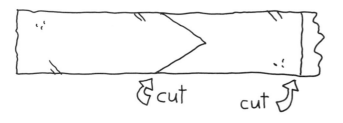

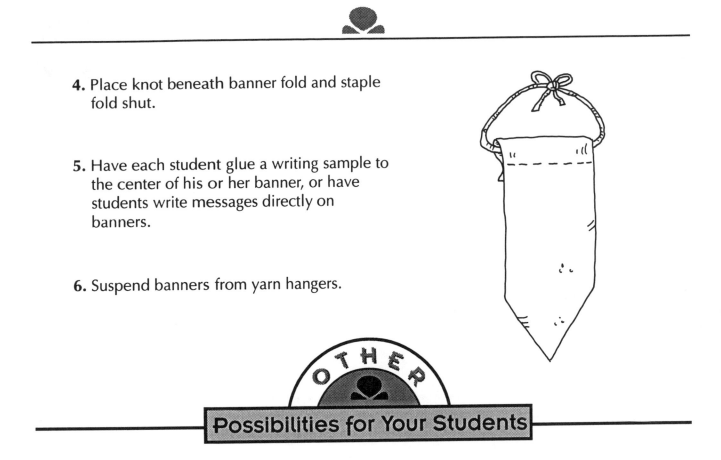

4. Place knot beneath banner fold and staple fold shut.

5. Have each student glue a writing sample to the center of his or her banner, or have students write messages directly on banners.

6. Suspend banners from yarn hangers.

OTHER
Possibilities for Your Students

- Slip a thin dowel through banner fold and tie ends of yarn to ends of dowel.

- Design other banner shapes, or simply fold the corners of a piece of construction paper over the shoulders of a hanger, staple in place and use to mount student writings.

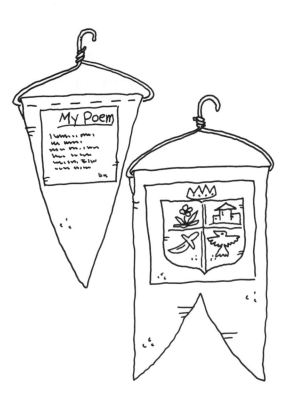

My Poem

- Use banners to showcase student-created coats of arms.

Book Jackets

☰ Materials:

• large pieces of light-colored construction paper • ruler

☰ Directions:

1. Hold paper horizontally and fold in half creating a vertical fold.

2. Using ruler, mark off 3″ vertical segments at either end of the paper and fold in to create flaps.

3. Have students use the jacket to design a new book cover for their favorite books.

4. The inside of the book jacket may be used to mount a book report or summary, so that when the book jacket is opened, the reader may learn more about the book featured on the cover.

5. Book jackets may be tacked to a bulletin board to create a display. Covers on display may be kept closed by tucking front flap behind book jacket.

OTHER Possibilities for Your Students

• Book jackets may be created to advertise books students have written and published in class.

Clothes Hanger Mobiles

Materials:

• wire clothes hangers • masking tape • construction paper • heavy weight yarn • hole puncher • scissors • index cards • glue

Directions:

1. Knot yarn to neck of each hanger and begin wrapping yarn around hangers. Press yarn closely together on hanger.

2. Transfer a piece of writing or a list of fascinating research facts to index cards.

3. Have students cut two construction paper shapes to accompany writing sample.

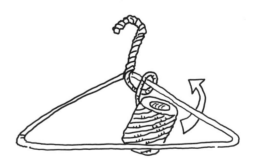

4. Use hole punch to create a hole at least 1/4 " down from the top of each shape and from the top of each index card.

5. Cut a piece of yarn into a number of descending lengths (e.g. 10", 8", 5"...), so that mobile pieces can hang freely. Cut one piece of yarn for each piece of paper to be hung.

6. Thread one piece of yarn through one hole in one of the pieces of paper and tie to the hanger. Try to achieve a balanced look.

7. Suspend your mobiles from classroom ceiling wires located in a breezy spot.

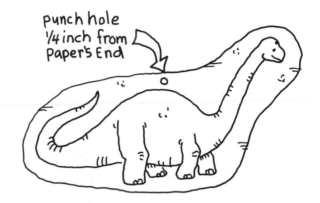

punch hole 1/4 inch from Paper's End

Possibilities for Your Students

• Squeeze glue along hanger edge. Lay the entire hanger on one piece of butcher paper. Add glue to other side of hanger. Cover with another piece of butcher paper. Let dry and cut out. Have students write directly on butcher paper thus creating "hang-able" handwritings.

Today our class went to the Public Library and then we had lunch at the park. It was great fun.

Crowns

Materials:

- crown patterns and extensions copied from pages 85, 86, and 87 • construction paper
- scissors • copy paper cut into strips approximately 2″ x 10″ • stapler • glue • sequins or glitter

Directions:

1. Trace crown patterns and extensions onto construction paper.

2. Use copy paper strips to have children record wishes, pledges, slogans, "Happy Birthday" salute, etc.

3. Have children cut out crown shapes. Staple each of these to extension bands that have been precut and stapled into circles fitted to the students' heads.

4. Decorate the crowns with glued on sequins or glitter. Let dry before wearing.

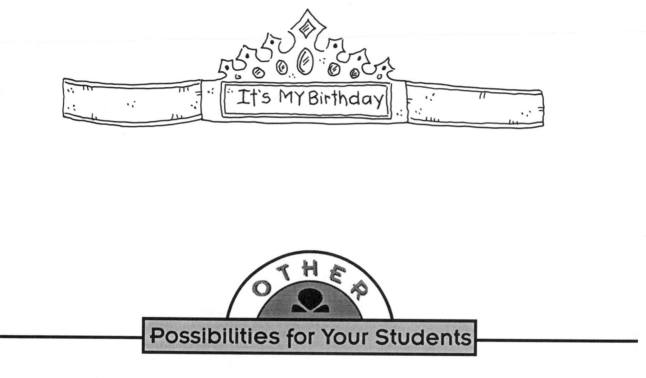

O T H E R

Possibilities for Your Students

- Have students design their own crowns.

- Decorate crowns with stapled-on paper faces to represent story characters. These make great "instant costumes" for play-acting.

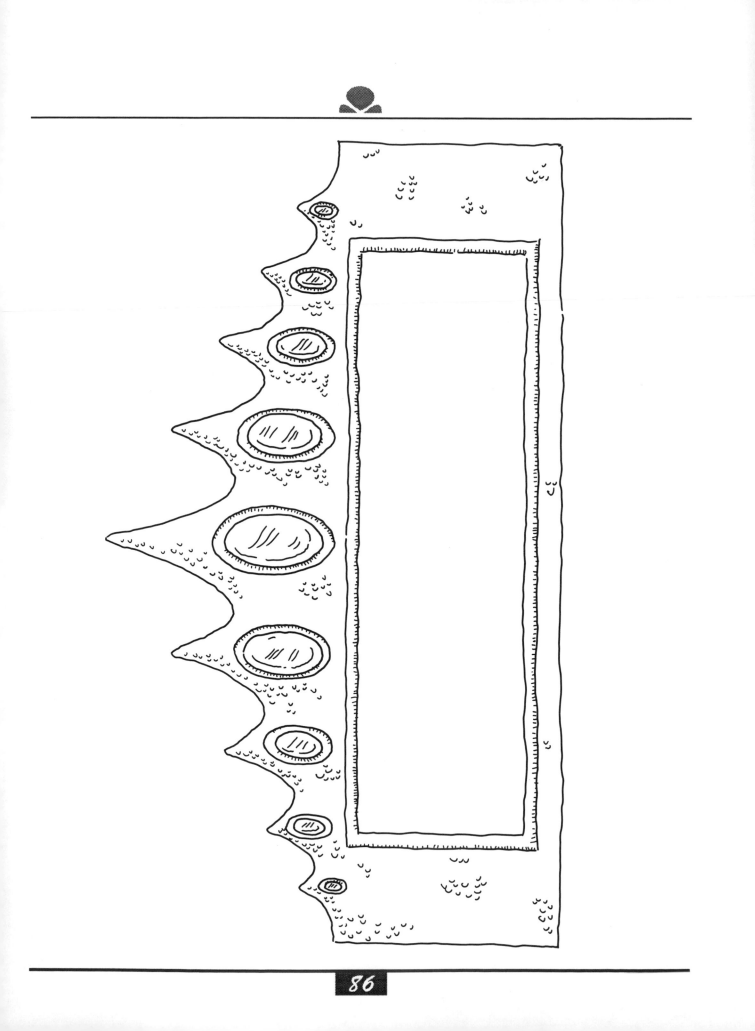

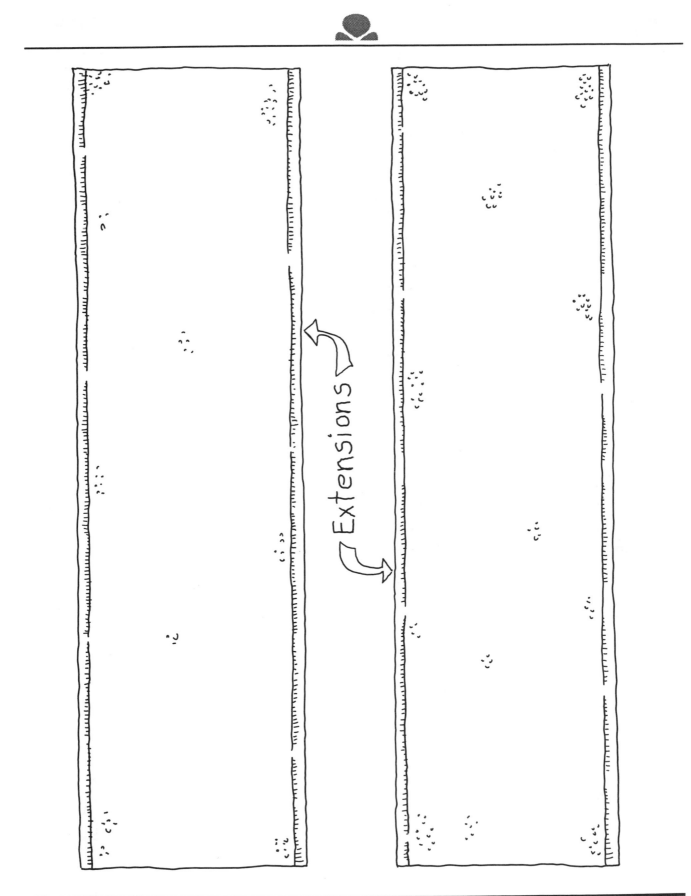

Extensions

Display Animals

Dear Santa,
I would like a set of
headphones for Christmas
and a new radio. I really
need them because I won't
disturb you and Dad with
my loud music. Thank You.

Materials:

• copies of the creature body and designs on pages 90 and 91 • discarded file folders or oaktag cut to 8 1/2" wide x 11" long and folded vertically • scissors • glue • small-size plain paper plates • yarn and glue-on googlie eyes to decorate creature faces

Directions:

1. Have students open file folder or oaktag and lay flat.

2. Then show students how to glue copy of creature body design to file folder or oaktag, aligning fold of copy to fold line on folder or oaktag; let dry.

3. Next, have students cut creature body where indicated on pattern, and then fold creature where indicated on pattern.

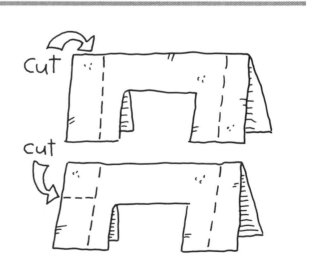

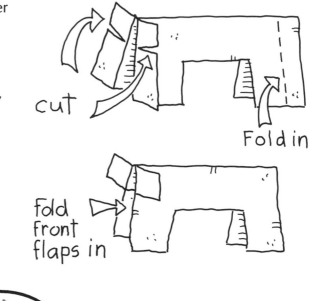

4. Have students glue face patterns or paper plates to front of animals and decorate with yarn, eyes and markers.

5. Invite students to use index cards to record writings (word-of-the-day, recipe, poetry, etc.) and clip or staple these to creature's back.

Possibilities for Your Students

- Each week remove the old composition and replace it with a new one. Make a new Display Creature each month.

- Glue googlie eyes on the face of the creature.

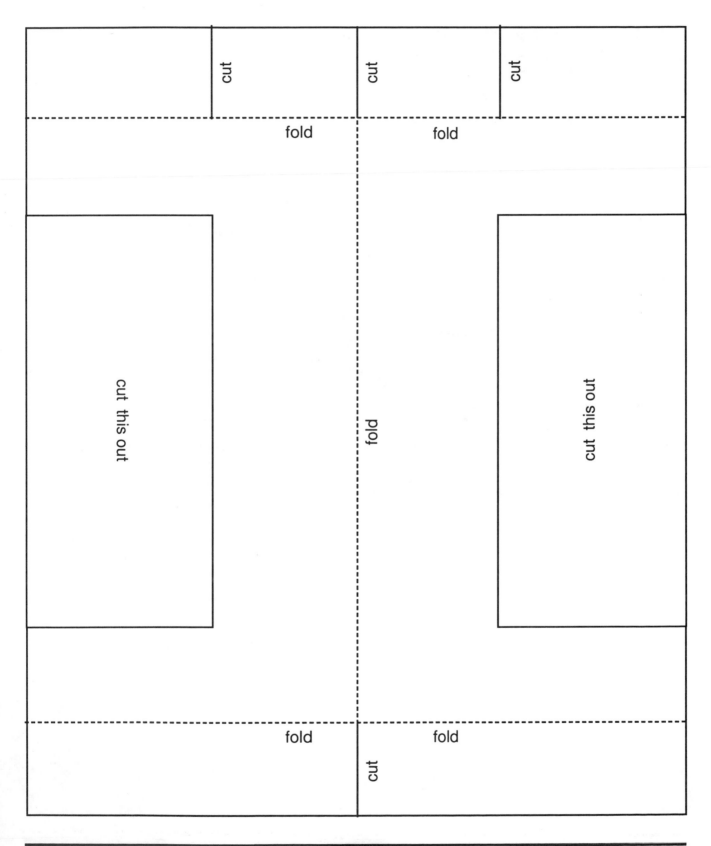

≡ Materials:

- copies of doorknob hanger patterns on page 94 • construction paper • glue • markers
- yarn

≡ Directions:

1. Provide students with copies of the doorknob hanger.

2. Have students use glue to mount their hangers on construction paper allowing a margin of construction paper to extend beyond edge of hanger. (Two hangers will fit on a regular-size piece of construction paper.)

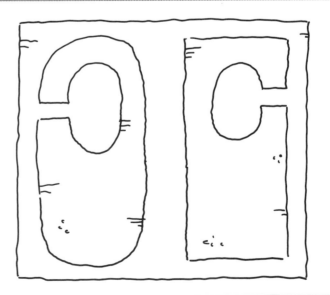

3. Brainstorm a list of possible messages, and then invite students to record their favorites on their hangers.

Possibilities for Your Students

- Instead of cutting a hole, use a matte knife to cut four crisscrossing lines at the top of a piece of construction paper.

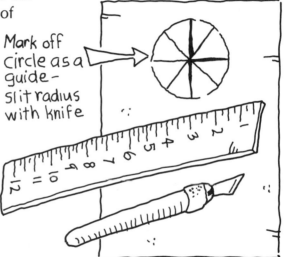

Mark off circle as a guide— slit radius with knife

- Decorate hangers to resemble vehicles or animals.

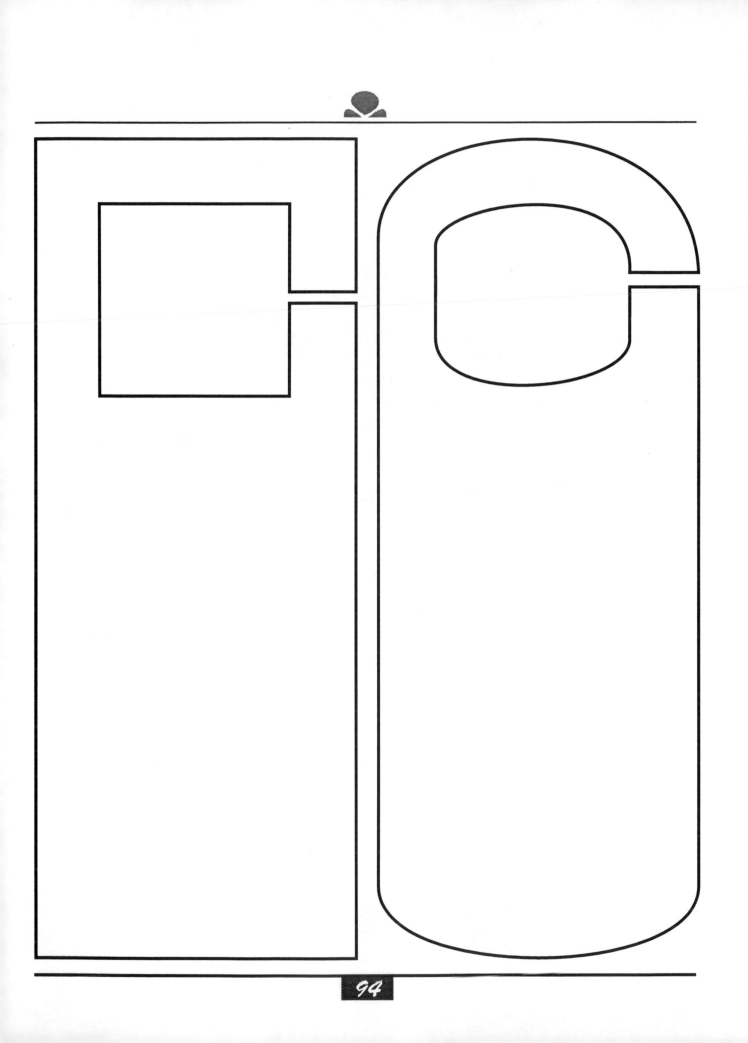

Fantastic Flat Kids

Materials:

• white or brown butcher paper •pencil • markers • scissors • tempera paints in primary and multicultural tints • yarn

Directions:

1. Assign each child a partner.

2. Have partners take turns lying on the paper so that one partner may trace the other. Children may pose in any way they wish, but open hands must extend sideways from arms stretched out above waistlines.

3. Have students use paints and yarn (for hair) to decorate their faces and bodies.

4. When dry, have students cut themselves out and then bend arms in at the elbows in order to paint other side of arms.

5. Mount dried bodies on the wall and attach pieces of student writings to paper hands.

Possibilities for Your Students

• Cut shirts, blouses, and jeans out of colorful wallpaper books.

• Show students how to make hair. Straight hair can be made by fringing construction paper that is about 1 1/2 to 2 inches wide.

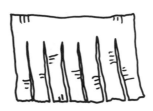

• Curly hair can be made with yarn or by cutting ribbon and pulling these across the sharp edge of a scissors. Hair can then be glued on the head.

Flowers

Materials:

• copies of the patterns on page 99 • scissors • glue • pad of small, removable sticky notes (trimmed to circular shapes, if desired)

Directions:

1. Have students color flowers and leaves as desired and then cut them out.

2. Have students use center of flowers to record one fabulous flower fact (or one bird fact, or one ecology tip, etc.).

3. Flowers, centers and leaves may then be stapled to paper stems of varying heights and arranged on a bulletin board to create a "Flowery Field of Facts."

4. Have students use markers to add other details (birds, clouds, sun, more flowers, etc) to the display.

Possibilities for Your Students

- Have students each make several flowers and stems. Tape these to a construction paper vase shape and mount the vase on a large sheet of construction paper of a contrasting color. Flower facts may then be recorded on the notes and posted on the flower centers.

Gabby Talkers

Materials:

• copies of patterns on page 102 • large-size craft sticks • googlie eyes (optional) • yarn (optional) • pencil • scissors • markers • glue

Directions:

1. Provide each student with a copy of the patterns on page 102.

2. Instruct students to use glue to mount this pattern page onto construction paper; let dry and cut out.

3. Have students fold and crease mouth piece in half as indicated.

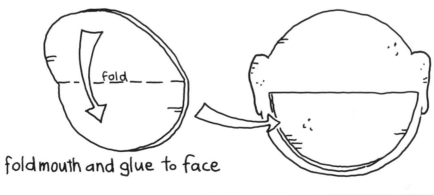

fold mouth and glue to face

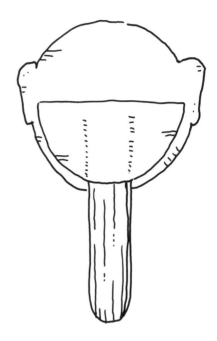

4. Have students glue tongue depressor to middle of chin. Stick should extend in at least 3".

5. Students should then glue mouth to lower half of face, aligning edges of circles together, and securing stick between papers.

6. Invite students to use markers, glued-on yarn and eyes to decorate faces.

7. Two-part messages (such as riddles, questions and answers, etc.) may be written on the outside and inside of the mouth pieces.

8. If desired, students may stand their "Gabby Talkers" into slits cut into inverted cup bottoms.

Possibilities for Your Students

• Cut two identical shapes from construction paper. Glue shapes together with craft stick sandwiched between shapes. Glue writings to front and back of stick puppets, or write directly on shapes.

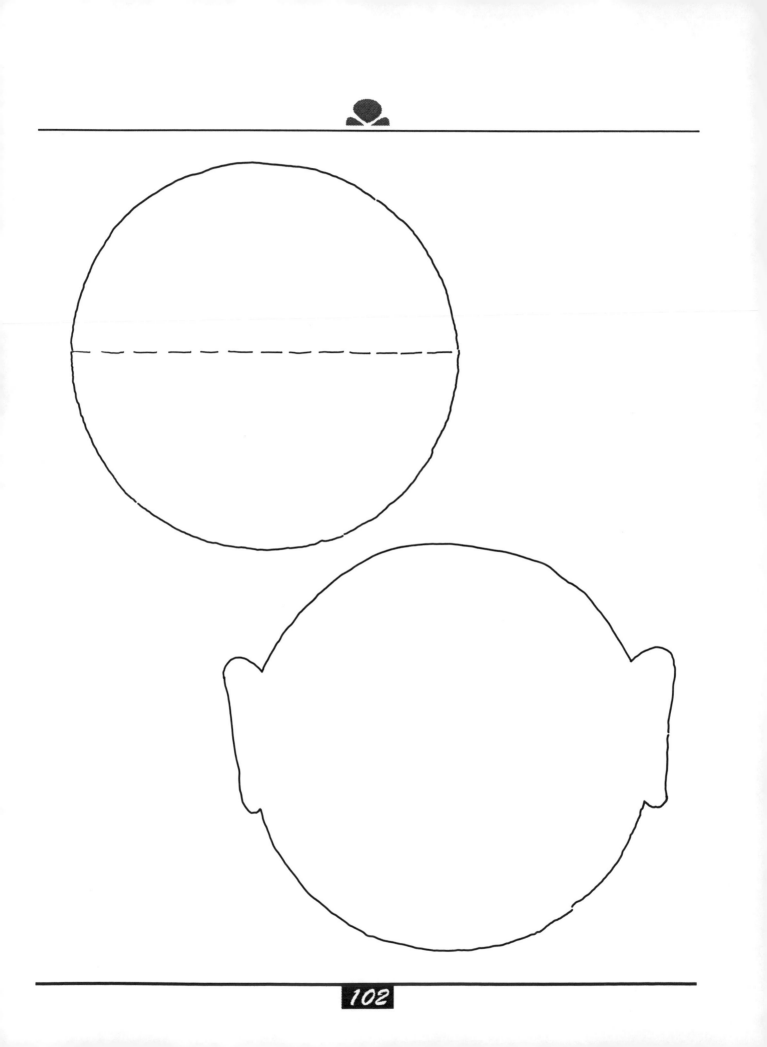

Materials:

• large and medium sized grocery sacks (with writing on only one side), • medium pointed black pens • felt tip markers • pencils

Directions:

Invite students to:

1. Fold the grocery sack shut if it is open. Then turn the sack so that the large empty side faces you. The grocery store's name should face down.

2. Plan where composition and illustration will go. Use a pencil to lightly pencil in your composition. Also sketch in your illustration very lightly. Remember once you start writing in black pen you won't be able to start over.

3. Write in your composition with a medium pointed black pen. Use felt tipped colored markers to draw your illustration.

4. On the front of the bag write only your first name and our school's name. (Depending on where the school is located, some parents may want their child's name left off the sack. In cases like this consider having students write their grade level and name of school.)

5. When you are finished, open your sack and set it in your hallway so that we will have a chance to see and read everyone's sack before it goes back to the grocery store to be distributed.

OTHER

Possibilities for Your Students

- Contact other types of stores that use paper sacks or bags.

Paper Tornadoes

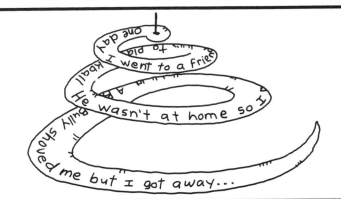

One day I went to a friend to play kball... He wasn't at home so I Billy shoved me but I got away...

≡ Materials:

• copies of spiral pattern on page 106 or on page 107 • scissors • yarn, cut into pieces 18" long • tape

≡ Directions:

1. Offer students copies of the pattern on page 106 or 107.

2. Demonstrate how to print messages on spirals by beginning to write at the center of the spiral and working out from there.

3. After students have written messages on their spirals, have students cut spirals out along lines as indicated.

4. Offer students the hole puncher and ask them to punch a hole through each of the dots indicated on the spiral.

5. Students should then tie one end of their yarn through the hole, and tie the other end to a ceiling wire, book case, desk chair, etc.

Possibilities for Your Students

• Have students cut their own hurricanes/tornadoes without a pattern. Experiment several times first. Be sure students keep at least one half inch wide area on each part of the spiral so that they will have room for their compositions.

• Try cutting inexpensive paper plates into hurricanes/tornadoes.

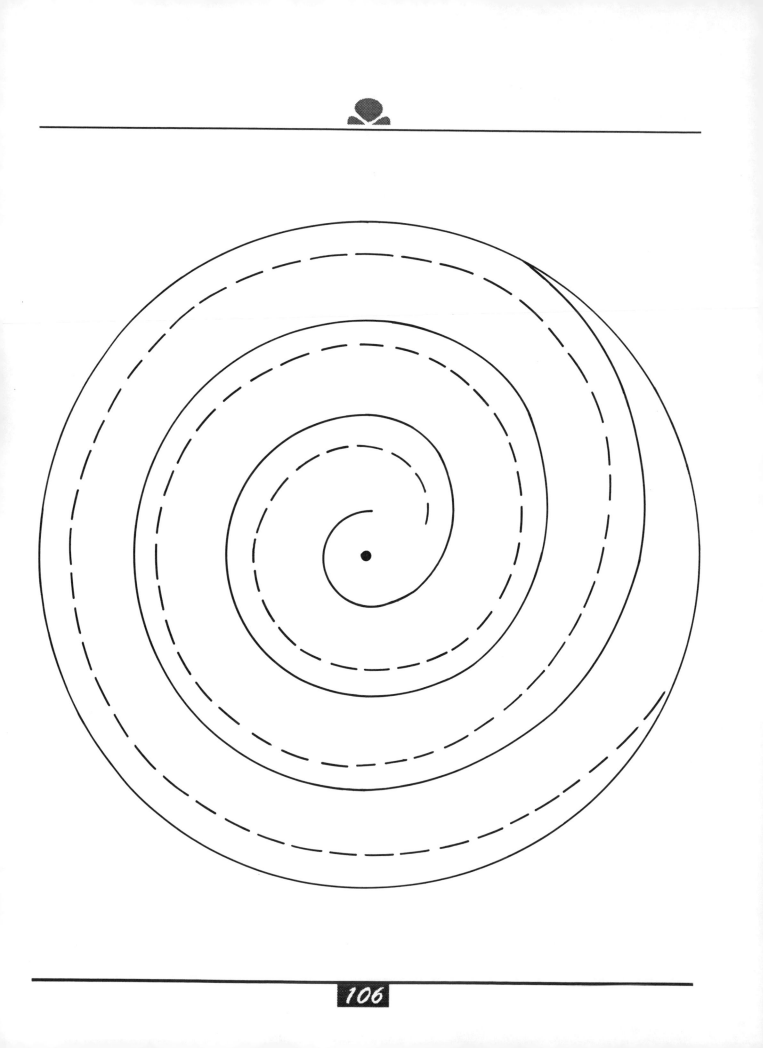

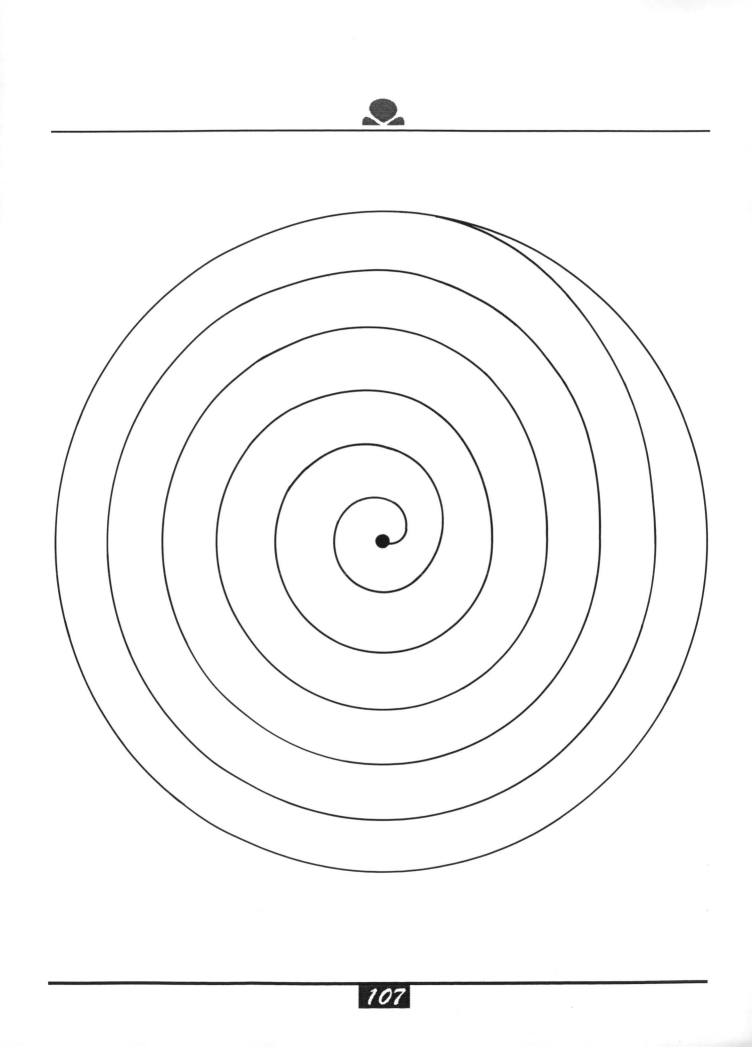

Magnetic Memo Clips

Materials:

- magnetic tape (available from craft supply stores) • wooden spring clothespins
- photographs or pictures cut from magazines • old file folders

Directions:

1. Mount photo or picture by gluing to file folder; let dry and trim folder to size of picture. (Save any left-over folder to use with other projects or for mounting more pictures for this project!)

2. Glue magnet strip to one side of clothespin (above spring) and let dry.

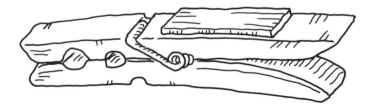

3. Glue photo or picture to other side of clothespin (above spring) and let dry.

4. Stick decorated clothes pin to magnet surface (chalkboard, metal file cabinet or kitchen appliance) and use to post written memos in school or at home.

5. Have students write a special message on a small piece of oaktag, such as "My Art Work" or "My Very Best." Glue one of these messages to each clothes pin and present (along with a piece of art work or writing) to parents as a gift to help showcase students' current and upcoming work.

- Have students draw a picture on some typing paper. Glue this to the rectangle in place of the magazine picture.

- Have students write a reminder on the construction paper such as "Praise Works Better than Criticism" or "I'm proud of this paper". Glue this to the rectangle. Use as a gift to parents. Of course the gift will include the student's composition.

Pops

≡ **M**aterials:

• construction paper • lined writing paper • scissors • tongue depressors • pencil • glue

≡ **D**irections:

1. Duplicate copies of the pattern for each student.

2. Trace the pattern on the construction paper two times.

3. Cut out two patterns.

4. Write your composition on one pattern. (If you want the students' compositions to attract attention, have them write on lined paper that is smaller than the head and then glue it on.)

5. Glue the tongue depressor to the other side of the pattern. The tongue depressor should protrude 1/2 to 3/4 of its length below the pattern.

6. Lay the other pattern over the tongue depressor and the back of the other pattern.

7. Draw, cut out, or glue construction paper on the pattern.

OTHER Possibilities for Your Students

- Decorate the Pops with yarn, buttons, wiggly eyes, glitter, ribbon, etc.

- Have students create their own shapes for the Pop.

- Make a Pop out of just one pattern piece. Instead of gluing a front and a back together, write the composition on the front of the Pop and tape the tongue depressor on to the back side.

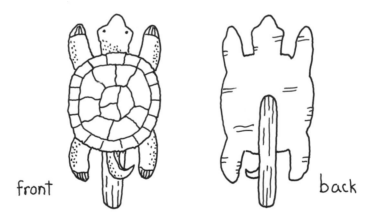

front   back

- Cut out a 3-5 part comic. Cut apart each section. Make 3-5 Pops and glue the comic to the front of the Pop and write your story or dialogue on the back of each Pop.

- Make personal fans. Cut a fan shape out of light weight tag board (old file folders). Students' compositions can be placed on both sides of the fan or on one side with a picture on the other side.

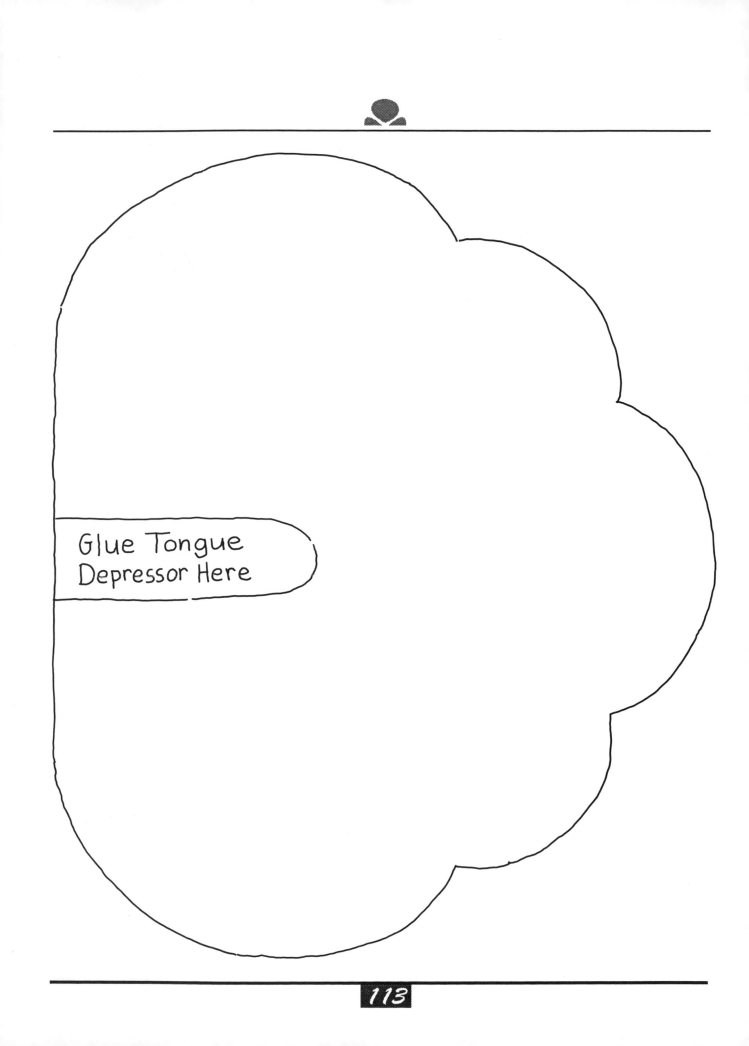

Segmented Stretchies

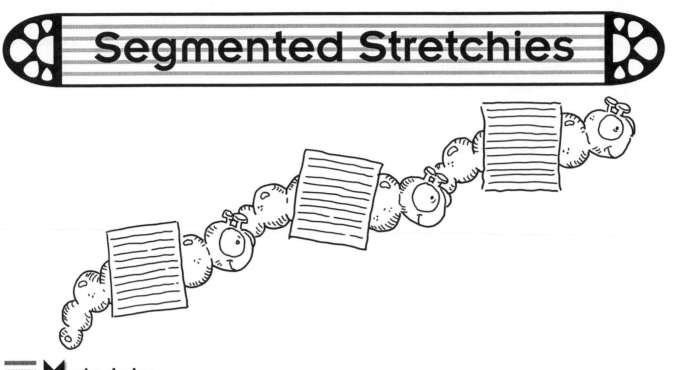

Materials:

- copies of the segment shapes on page 115 • scissors • tape or stapler • crayons and markers

Directions:

1. Place supply of cut-out segments into an envelope.

2. Attach envelope to a bulletin board.

3. Also, attach first segment with story starter (Once upon a time...) to bulletin board.

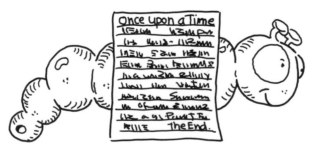

4. Invite students to use segments to record additions to story line. Completed segments may be taped or stapled to end of display.

5. Challenge students to see how long they can make their "Stretchie" stretch.

Single String Mobiles

Materials:

- yarn or string cut to 30″ pieces • copies of the shapes on pages 118 and 119.
- construction paper • scissors • glue

Directions:

1. Offer each student two copies of the shapes on pages 118 and 119.

2. Have students cut out shapes along lines as indicated.

3. Have students arrange shapes face down, 3″ apart, in descending size order.

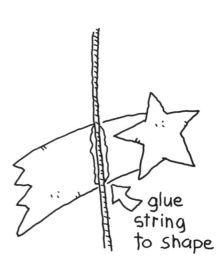

glue string to shape

4. Have students lay yarn or string over center of shapes (so that 8″ of yarn extends beyond the top of the largest shape) and spread glue over shapes.

5. Students should then cover bottom shapes and yarn or string with matching shapes pressed in place, right-side-up.

6. Have students use the shapes to record descriptive words, related verbs, stories, etc.

7. Mobiles may then be taped to doorways or windows, or suspended from ceiling wires.

Possibilities for Your Students

• Have children design their own shapes.

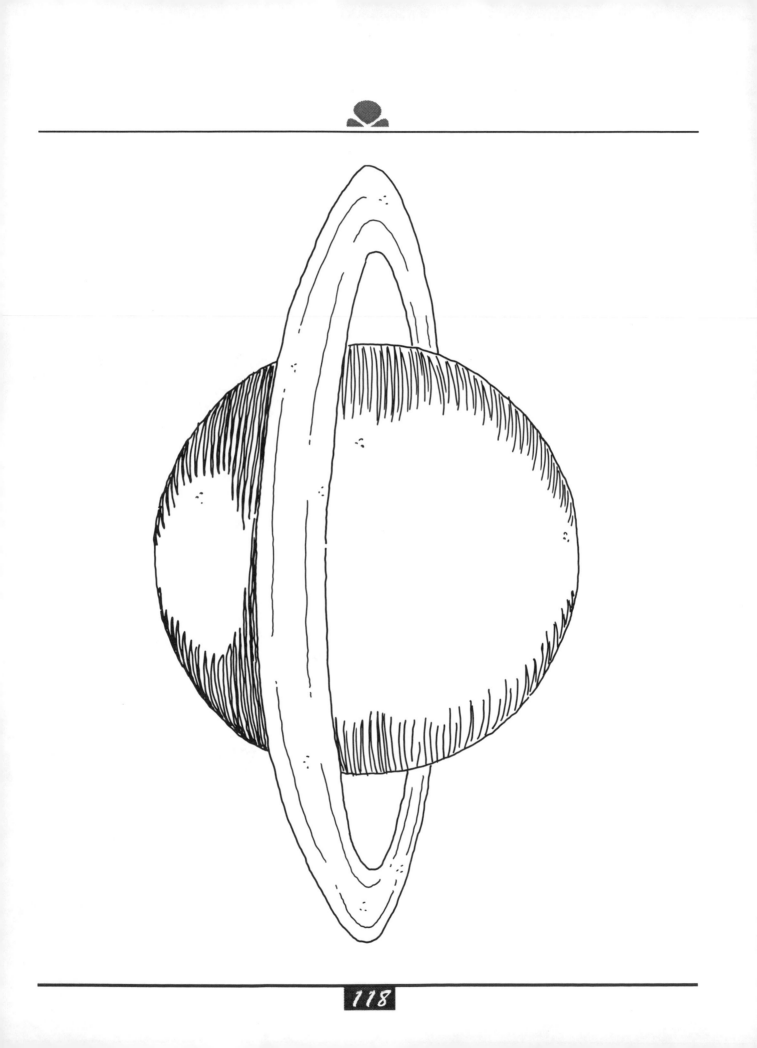

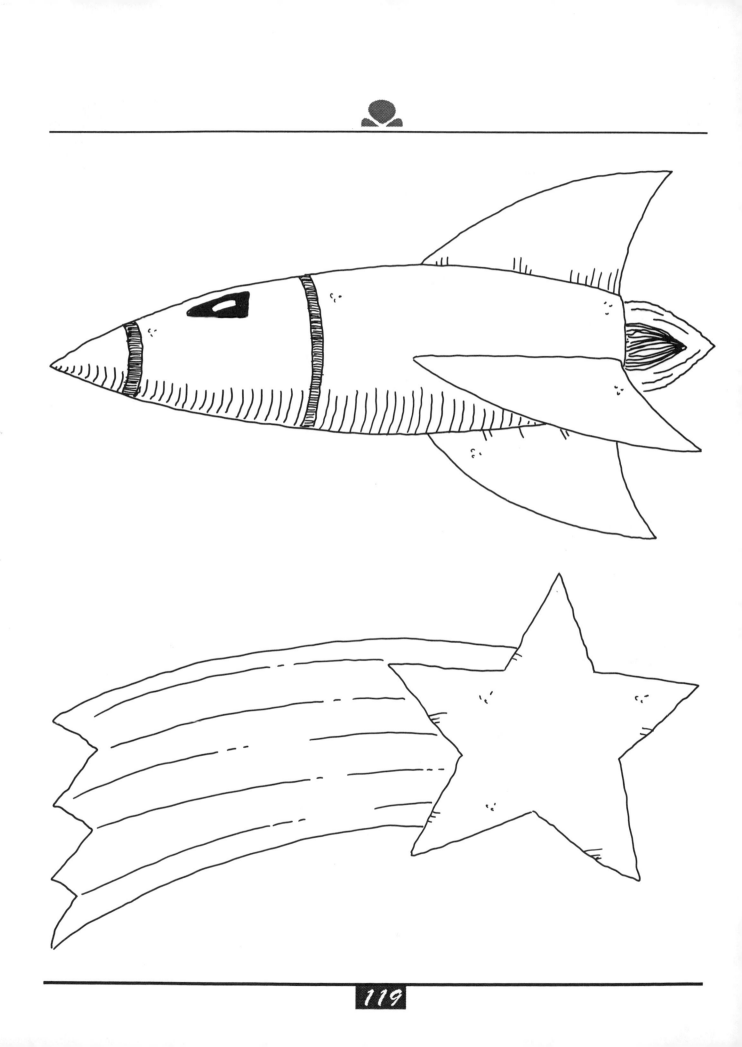

Sun Visors

Materials:

• copies of sun visor pattern on page 122 • elastic thread • scissors • glue • backing paper such as oaktag, lightweight cardboard or discarded file folders • crayons and neon-colored felt-tipped markers

Directions:

1. Provide students with copies of sun visor pattern. Have them cut out the pattern and glue onto backing paper. Let dry and trim paper to size of pattern.

2. Punch holes in visor where indicated, and then fold ends down along fold lines.

3. Help students tie elastic thread through holes, adjusting individual threads to fit around each student's head.

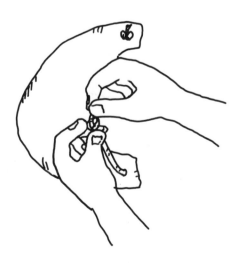

4. Invite students to decorate top of visors with slogans, sayings, exclamations, jokes, riddles, etc. Reserve undersides for recording students' names.

Possibilities for Your Students

- Instead of using yarn, buy some black elastic string sold at fabric stores. While this costs more, students like how simple the sun visors are to remove and replace on their heads. Cut a 5 inch piece of elastic. Attach each end of the elastic with staples.

- To make the Sun Visors more durable laminate them after students have added their information in step two.

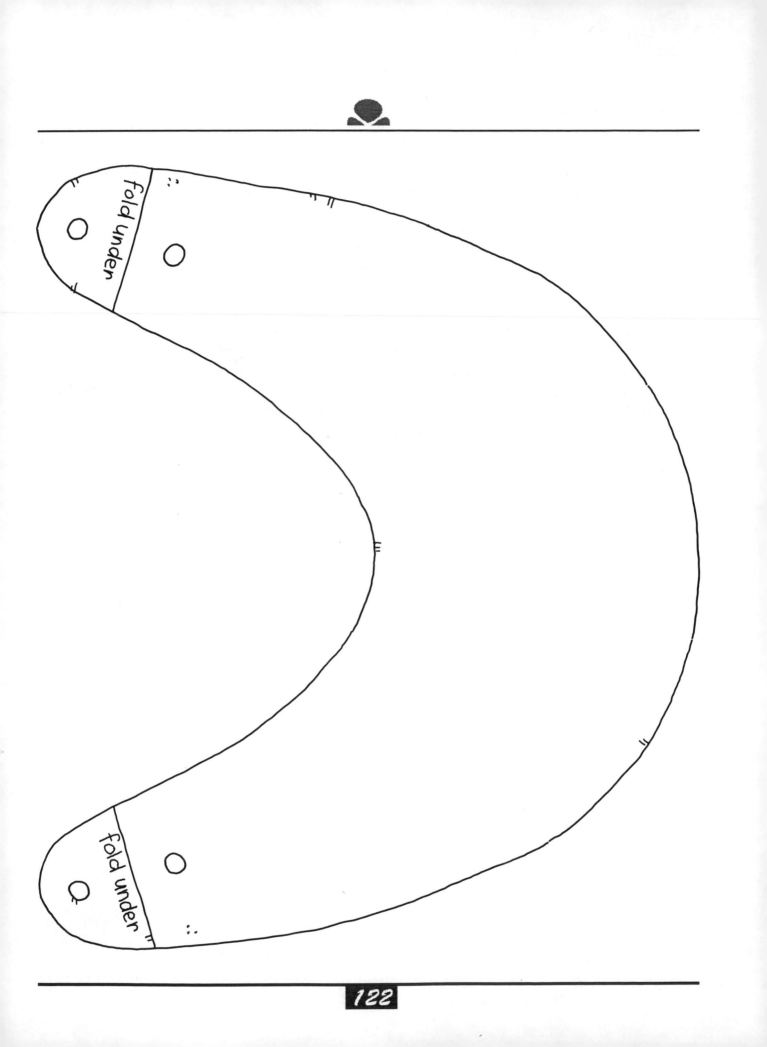

fold under

fold under

Tents

Materials:

- construction paper • writing paper • glue • scissors • tape • ruler

Directions:

1. Hold a piece of construction paper horizontally and fold in half from left to right; crease fold.

2. Open paper up and draw a vertical margin 1 1/2 " in from the left and right hand edge of the paper.

3. Fold paper in along lines to create flaps.

4. Halfway down on each flap, make a 2/3" cut from edge of paper to fold line.

5. Fold tent again and lock paper together at slits. Place tape along slitted side to hold closed.

6. Have students mount (glue or tape) writing to either side of tent and stand to display.

7. Experiment with tents of various sizes by adjusting the size of the folded flaps.

Possibilities for Your Students

- Make different sized tents.

Materials:

- construction paper (9" x 12") • scissors • glue • staplers

Directions:

1. Have students stack two pieces of construction paper together and hold horizontally. Students should then fold paper from left to right creating a vertical folds.

2. Have students open their papers and cut along crease, thus creating four pieces of paper (4 1/2 " x 6").

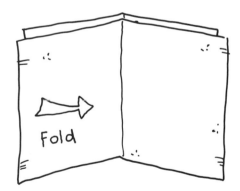

3. Show students how to hold cut pieces horizontally in order to glue writing samples to one side of each of three pieces of construction paper. If writing samples are short, students may use remaining space for illustrations. (Writing samples may or may not be related to each other. If one piece of writing is to be divided among the three faces of the corral, The writing should be arranged so it can be read in sequence by turning the corral clockwise.)

4. To assemble corrals, have students stack two pieces of the construction paper together back-to-back and staple two of the shorter ends together.

5. Students should then carefully open the unstapled edge of the corral and align the two open edges with the edges of the third paper to create a triangle shape. Staple this third paper to the first two along the edges that meet.

6. Corrals are free-standing or may be hung from three pieces of yarn attached to the three corral corners and tied together in the middle.

Possibilities for Your Students

- More colorful corrals can be made from wallpaper from old wallpaper books. When you use wallpaper you will have to staple your compositions on instead of gluing them on.

- To make your corrals sturdier use tag board or old file folders instead of construcion paper. If you want a more finished look, slide plastic report binders over the stapled edges of a corral. Cut excess plastic off with sharp scissors.

- To make taller corrals use the same 4 1/2" sheets but staple them along the long sides instead of the short sides. Corrals can also be make from different sided pieces of paper such as squares 5 1/2" by 5 1/2" or circles with 5 1/2" diameter.

- Instead of making a three sided corral make a four sided one. It will hold lots more information.

Tube Dudes

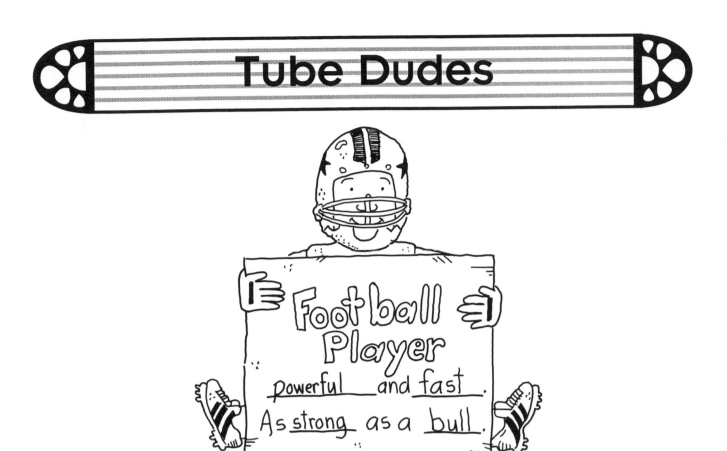

Football
Player
powerful and fast.
As strong as a bull.

☰ Materials:

- empty toilet paper tubes • Tube Dude pattern on page 129 • construction paper
- scissors • glue • tape • index cards • stapler

☰ Directions:

Duplicate and distribute Tube Dude patterns. Invite students to:

1. Color the face of your Tube Dude.

2. Cut out the head, arms, and feet of your Tube Dude.

3. Glue the head, arms, and legs on to another sheet of construction paper to make it stronger. Be sure they do not overlap.

4. Again cut out the head, arms, and feet of your Tube Dude.

5. Put glue on the rectangular piece of construction paper and wrap it around the toilet tube. Use tape to keep it on until the glue dries.

wrap 4½"x 7" rectangle and tape to roll.

6. Wrap the feet around the base of the toilet tube and glue them on. Wrap the arms about one inch from the top of the toilet tube and glue them on.

7. Now turn the Tube Dude to face you. Glue its face at the top of the front side of the toilet tube.

8. Hold the index card with your composition on it next to the two hands of your Tube Dude. Staple the index card to each hand of your Tube Dude. Make sure the face still shows.

Possibilities for Your Students

- While tube holders have been around for a long time, the Paper Tube Zoo by Joy Evans & Jo Ellen Moore, (1988) has many unusual types such as kangaroos, dinosaurs, crocodiles, elephants, hippos, cows, pigs, lambs, bats, etc.

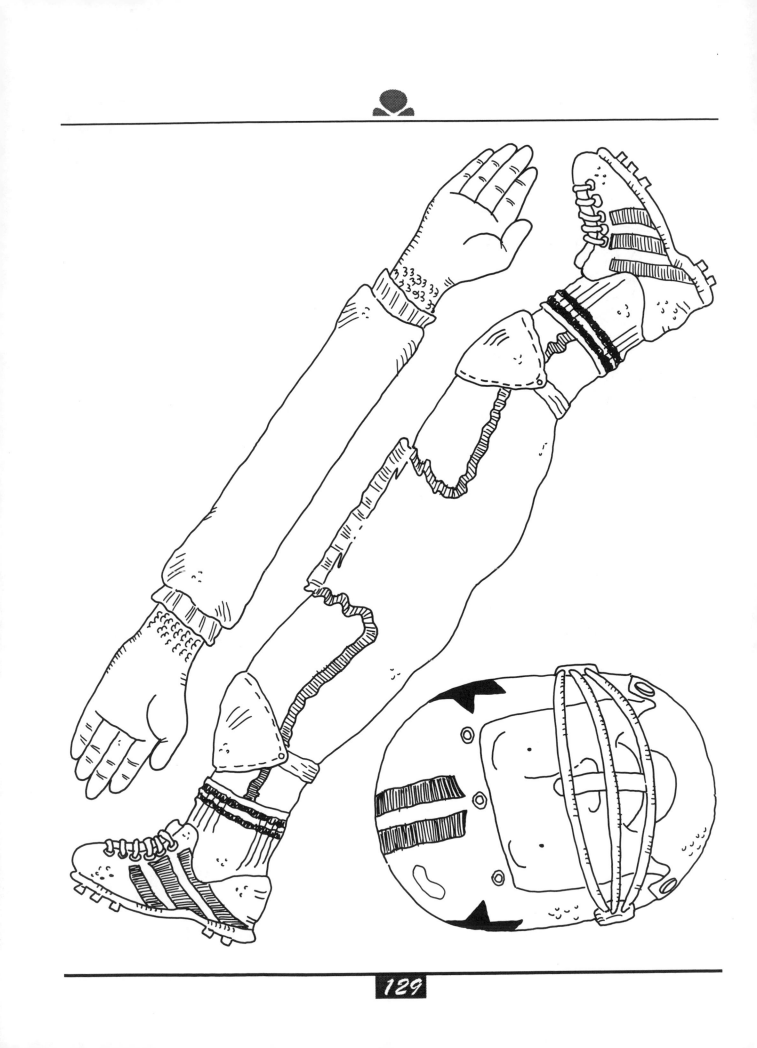

Wanted Posters

≡ Materials:

- Wanted Poster pattern on page 132 • pencil

≡ Directions:

1. Decide who is wanted and for what. Add these to a blank wanted poster.

2. Draw a picture of who or what is wanted in the small rectangle.

3. Now add a written description of the person or thing to your wanted poster.

4. Finally add how much reward will be given for the capture of this person or thing.

5. Tack your wanted poster to a bulletin board or a tree for others to read.

Possibilities for Your Students

- Glue on a recent photograph or a picture from a magazine instead of drawing a picture.

- Instead of taping or nailing the posters to a wall, make 10 copies of your poster and hand them out to people. If you are going to duplicate the posters make the drawings in pencil not crayon or markers. Otherwise the pictures will not copy well.

WANTED

Who: _____

Wanted for: _____

Description: _____

_____

_____

_____

_____

REWARD

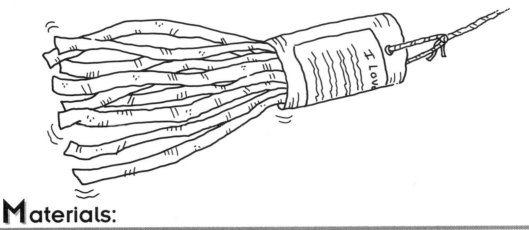

Materials:

• construction paper • rolled crepe paper streamers cut to 16" each • pieces of yarn or string cut into pieces 18" long • glue • hole punch • stapler

Directions:

1. Use glue to mount writing sample on construction paper.

2. When dry, help students fashion paper into cylinders. Tape and staple in place.

3. Have students use the hole punch to punch two holes across from each other 2" down from the top of the cylinder.

4. Instruct students to thread one piece of yarn or string through each hole, and to tie string ends together at the top.

5. Help students tape six or seven crepe paper streamers to inside bottom of cylinder.

6. Hang in a breezy spot.

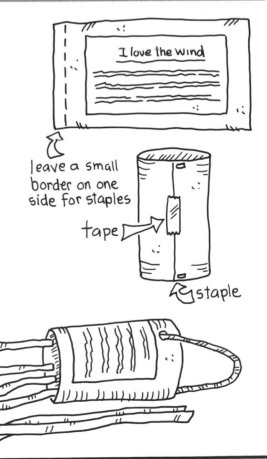

I love the wind

leave a small border on one side for staples

tape

staple

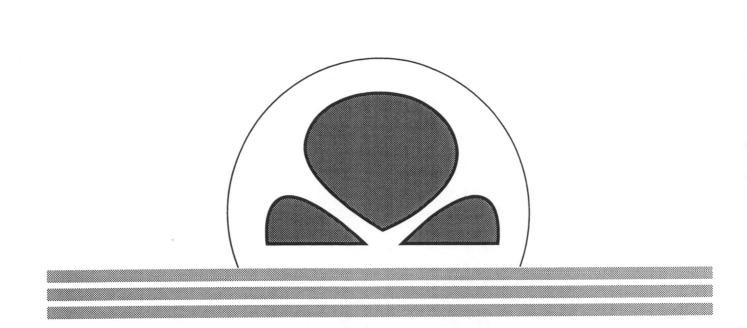

Special Writing Tools and Papers

Adding Machine Tape

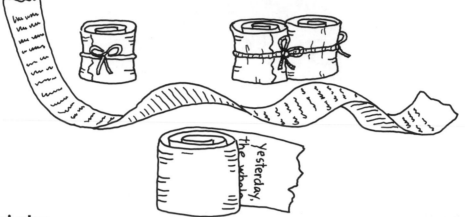

Materials:

• 5 to 8 rolls of adding machine tape • rulers or yardsticks • pencils• scissors • rubber band • yarn

Directions:

1. Have each student measure and cut 3' of tape from a roll.

2. Have students hold tape vertically or horizontally and use to record stories or messages.

3. Show students how to use pencil to start rolling completed writings up tight. Remove pencil from rolled tape and tie closed with yarn or rubber band.

- Have students attach paper heads and feet (or other paper shapes) to either ends of the tape, and display around the class.

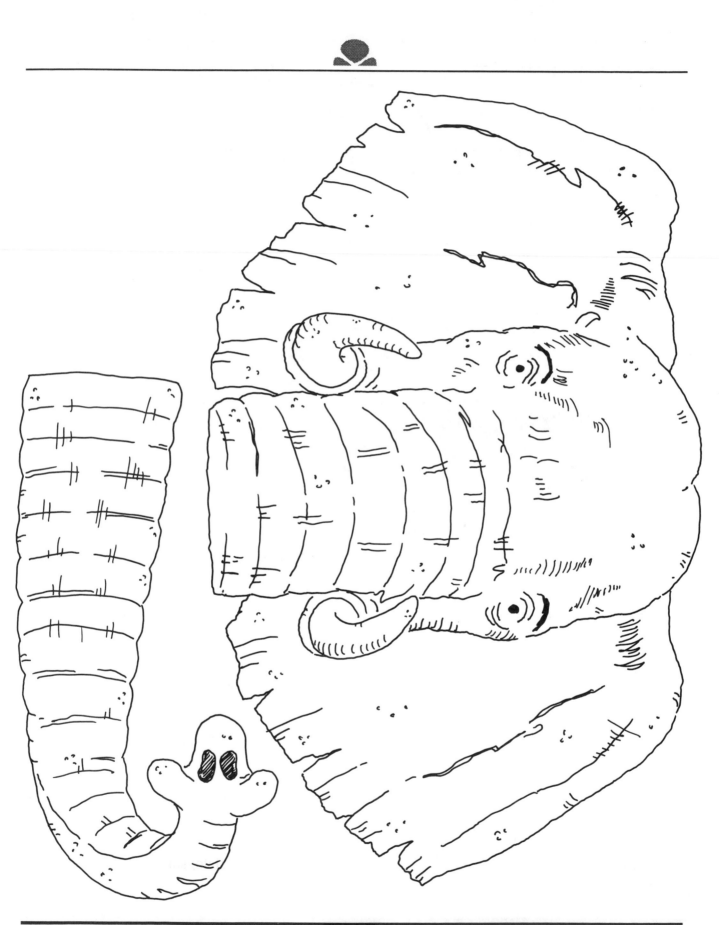

Birch Bark Stationery

Materials:

- strips of birch bark • ball point pens

Directions:

1. Have students break or peel bark pieces from a birch tree. (Use only the outermost layer which will peel off easily without damaging the tree.)

2. Have students write directly on the bark

3. Display writings together on a table.

Possibilities for Your Students

- Provide students with other natural writing instruments such as slate, sand in a shallow tub, etc.

Collage Writing

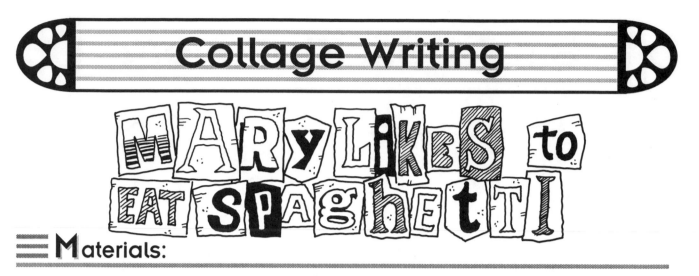

Materials:

• magazines • scissors • glue stick • construction paper • 26 sandwich bags, each labeled with one pair of upper and lower case alphabet letters • pencil or pen

Directions:

1. Tell students that you are going on a letter hunt.

2. Then, attach paper bags to a bulletin board, or tape them to the front of a chalk tray. Label each bag with one alphabet letter.

3. Have students spend time hunting and clipping individual alphabet letters to place into bags.

4. Have students glue down individual letters to create messages on the construction paper. When letter supplies run low, encourage students to write out any letter they need that is not available for gluing and then encourage them to clip more letters for future use!

Possibilities for Your Students

• Cut out words from the headlines of newspapers instead of magazines.

Good Graffiti

Materials:

- craft or butcher paper • bulletin board • markers • tempera paints and brushes

Directions:

1. Cover a large bulletin board with craft or butcher paper.

2. Paint a title such as "Write Now!" at the top of the display.

3. Invite students to "fill the wall with writing."

4. Encourage students to sign and illustrate their contributions.

I like to ride my bicycle in the rain.

• Post large theme-inspired paper shapes around the room to encourage theme-related writings.

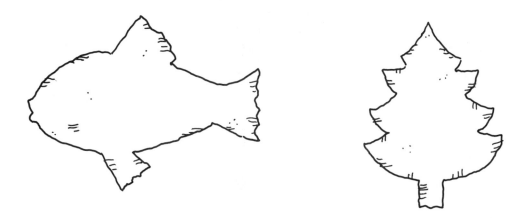

• Use an over head projector to create silhouettes of students' heads on white paper. Have students cut out silhouettes and use to record words that describe them and their interests.

Leather-Look Hides

The Feast
Late one evening Morning Song walked to the river. By the river stood a black buffalo. Morning Song took out her bow and fitted an arrow in it. Zoom went her arrow. All alone she skinned the buffalo, as she thought about the feast tonight.

Materials:

- brown grocery bags or butcher paper • scissors • markers

Directions:

1. Have students cut bags or butcher paper into hide shapes measuring approximately 9" x 9" as suggested by illustration.

2. Show students how to crumple and re-crumple paper until it is soft and pliable.

3. Suggest that students use hides to record stories or poems related to the great outdoors.

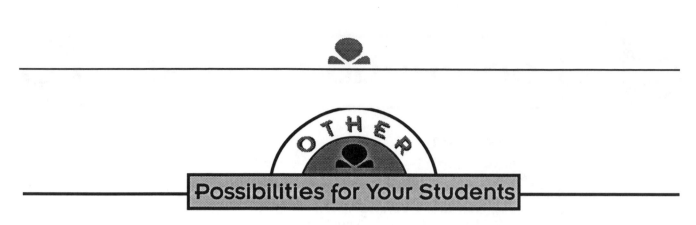
- Explore Native American pictographic symbols with students, then have them use the hides to display original pictograph stories.

friendly camp	Lake	hear	night
canoe	camp	fish	mountain
bravest	blanket	see	stars
talk together	lightning	little brave	rain

Overhead Transparencies

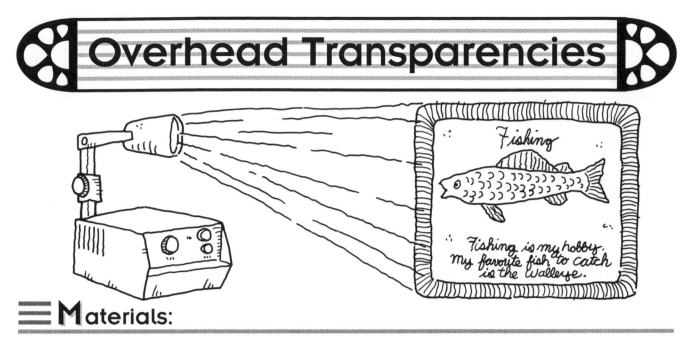

Materials:

• overhead transparencies • overhead projector • office machine designed to create overhead transparencies • copy machine • movie screen or wall covered with white craft paper

Directions:

1. Make copies of student writings on copy machine.

2. Use copies of student writings to create transparencies on an overhead projector.

3. Have willing students read their writings aloud to the class from the overhead image projected onto the screen or onto the wall.

Possibilities for Your Students

• Add a picture to your composition, before you make the transparency. Pencil or fine line drawings work the best.

• If you want to save students' compositions, give each student a transparency holder and show them how to tape in the transparency.

• If time or money is a problem, have students make temporary transparencies with grease pencils or colored felt markers.

Stickers

S~s~s~super
S~s~s~special !

e need
I can

for
rake
me

Materials:

- typing paper • newspaper • white non-toxic school (e.g., Elmer's) glue • white vinegar
- almond extract (Try other flavors too.) • small bowl or jar • spoon • paint brushes
- small plastic plates or bowls • felt tipped markers • magazine pictures • scissors • spatula

Directions:

Before class, use a paper cutter to cut out squares of typing paper in the desired size. Some sizes your students might try are 1 1/2" x 3 1/2", 3" x 3", 3" x 5", and 4" x 5".

Let students watch as you combine 1 cup white glue, 1/2 cup white vinegar, and three or four drops of almond extract. Mix well. Pour a small amount on to small bowls or plates for students to use.

Give students guidance as to appropriate and inappropriate places to stick stickers.

Invite students to:

1. Write your composition on to one of these sheets of paper. If desired, draw or cut out a small picture and glue it beside your composition.

2. Lay one sheet of newspaper on your desk.

3. Turn the writing side of your sticker down.

4. Paint on a very thin coat of the sticker formula on the back of it. Let this dry and then paint on second coat of the sticker formula.

5. When this coat is completely dry, cut off the edges that have curled. If there is room, now is the time to cut your sticker into a special shape.

6. Trade stickers with your friends. Lick and stick the stickers.

Codes

Pencil Wrap

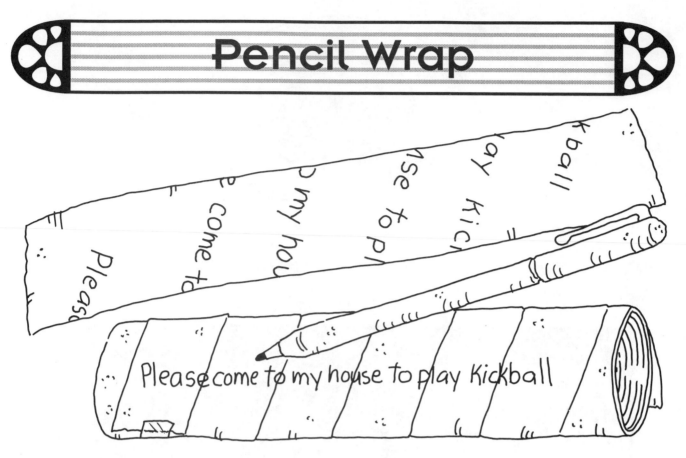

Please come to my house to play Kickball

Materials:

• empty paper towel tubes • tape • adding machine tape • pencils or fine-tipped markers

Directions:

1. Tape adding machine tape to one end of each tube.

2. Have students coil adding machine tape around tube without overlapping tape edges and without allowing tube to be exposed through any gaps.

3. Have students tape end of paper in place and then write message along the side of each wrapped tube.

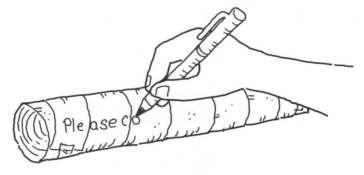

4. Students then untape and unwind the adding machine tape from tube, and trade messages with each other.

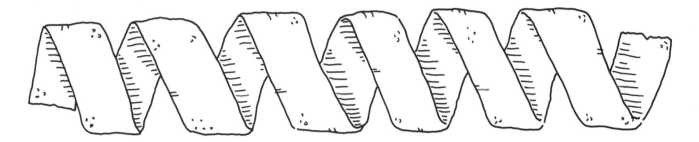

5. Help students as they work to rewind and decipher wrapped messages.

Possibilities for Your Students

- Encourage students to learn about different types of secret codes by reading books such as *Secret Codes* by Helen Jill Fletcher (New York: Watts, 1980).

Secret Carbon Paper Messages

Today is
Friday.

Thank goodness!

≡ Materials:

• carbon paper • copy paper • paper clips • pencils • mirror (large enough to reflect paper)

≡ Directions:

1. Instruct students to place carbon paper shiny side up on desk.

2. Have students cover carbon paper with two pieces of copy paper. Papers should be lined up and held together at top and at sides with paper clips.

3. Invite students to use pencils to write or draw on top sheet of paper. Students should press hard.

I like writing secret messages to my many girl friends at school

4. When done, have students remove clips and see where secret message appears.

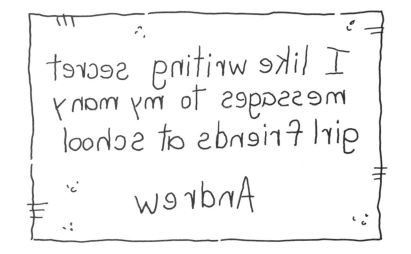

5. Have students try to read secret messages.

6. Show students what happens when each message is held up to the mirror.

7. Display original messages and secret messages together (but not next to each other) on a bulletin board display—Are children able to match original and secret messages?

Secret Crayon Messages

Materials:

• white copy paper • clean white crayons • water color paints • paintbrush

Directions:

1. Have students use crayons to write or draw a message on the copy paper. Remind students to press firmly.

2. Have students trade papers.

3. Invite students to paint over their classmates' message using a dark shade of watercolor paint in order to make secret messages appear.

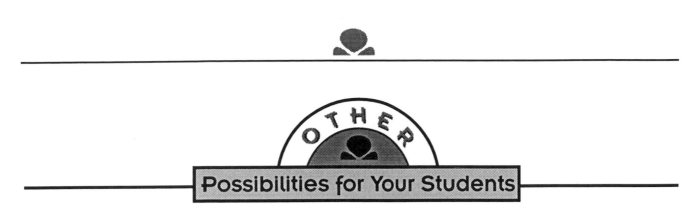

OTHER Possibilities for Your Students

- To learn more about different types of secret codes, ask your librarian to help you find books such as *How to Write Codes and Send Secret Messages* by John Peterson (New York: Scholastic Inc., 1966).

- Have students write a question at the top of a sheet of paper and the answer below.

Top Secret Decoder

Materials:

- copies of decoders and slider strips located on page 156 • construction paper • scissors
- tape • glue • clear, self-adhesive paper (optional but nice) • paper clips

Directions:

1. Provide each student with a copy of the decoders and slider strips on page 156.

2. Have students use glue to mount entire page onto construction paper and let dry.

3. If possible, cover front of page with clear, self-adhesive paper.

4. Have students cut apart the decoders and the sliders.

5. Show students how to lay the two alphabet and the two number strips with ends overlapping as indicated in the illustration. Tape overlapping ends together so that no space is apparent between the numbers or between the letters.

A B C D E F G H I
T U V W X Y Z
O P Q

6. Cut slits in either end of children's decoders and slip one alphabet and one number strip into each set of slits.

Kayla's Top Secret Code Slider

A B C D E F G H I J K L M N O P Q R S T U V W X Y Z

CUT
HERE

CUT
HERE

7. Have children each choose one favorite secret letter on their decoders. By moving each slider so that the A on the alphabet slider or the 1 on the number slider is beneath the chosen letter, students automatically assign all the other letters on the decoder a secret code letter or number. (Hint: Once students have decided on a code, a small piece of tape or paper clips can keep their sliders from slipping.)

8. Have children test out their decoders by writing their own names and simple messages in code as shown in the illustration. Remind students that only the decoder that helped them create the secret message can help them decode it.

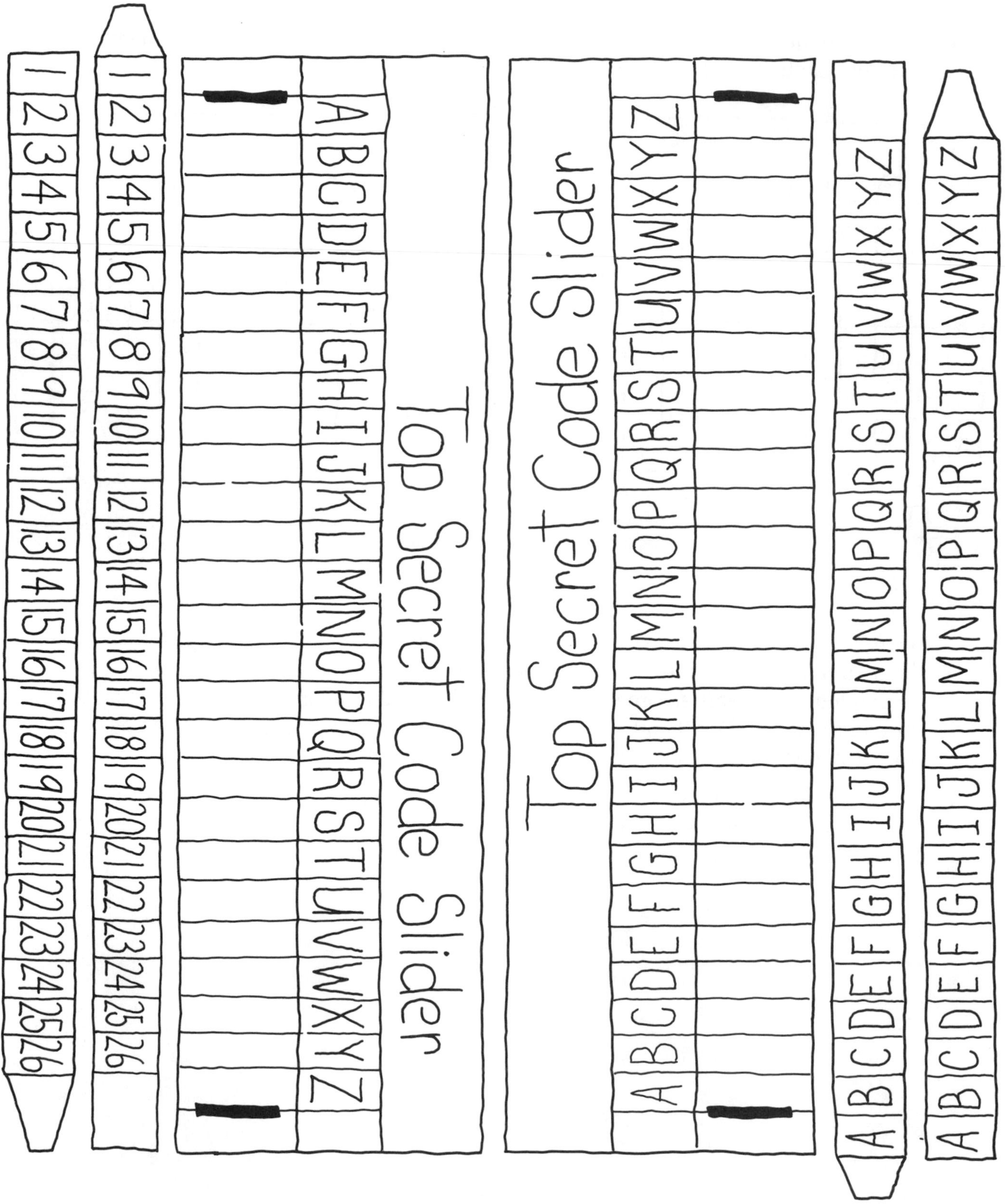

Top Secret Code Slider

Top Secret Code Slider

ABCDEFGHIJKLMNOPQRSTUVWXYZ

ABCDEFGHIJKLMNOPQRSTUVWXYZ

ABCDEFGHIJKLMNOPQRSTUVWXYZ

ABCDEFGHIJKLMNOPQRSTUVWXYZ

1 2 3 4 5 6 7 8 9 10 11 12 13 14 15 16 17 18 19 20 21 22 23 24 25 26

1 2 3 4 5 6 7 8 9 10 11 12 13 14 15 16 17 18 19 20 21 22 23 24 25 26

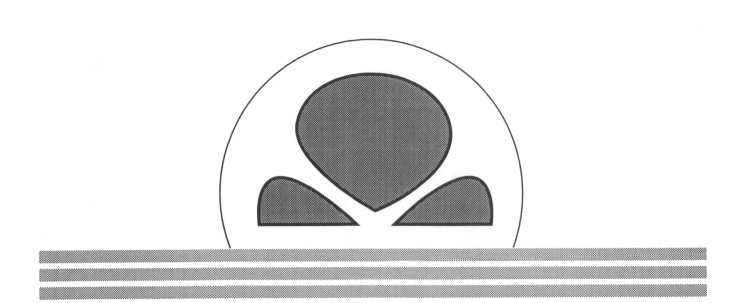

Miscellaneous

Banded Finger Puppets

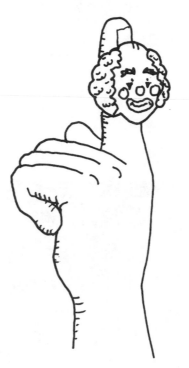

Materials:

- construction paper • cardboard or tag board • scissors • tape or stapler

Directions:

Invite students to:

1. Cut out a face or draw one on a 2″ by 2″ square. Make sure the face is at least 1 1/2″ high.

2. Cut out the face. Then glue the face on to a small piece of cardboard. Again, cut out the face.

3. Cut out a 1″ by 3″ piece of construction paper. This will be the band that will go around your finger.

4. Fold the band in half.

fold here

5. Staple the face to the middle of the folded band.

6. Wrap both ends of the band around your finger.

7. Hold the band snug on your finger and get someone to cut off the ends of the band that you don't need.

8. Finally tape the shortened ends together so the puppet is snug on your finger.

Bookmarks

This book marker is magic...
It can take you to any place
and any time you want to go.

Materials:

- copies of the bookmarks on page 162 • construction paper • glue • hole punch
- scissors • 1/4" wide ribbon cut into 10" long pieces

Directions:

1. Supply students with copies of the bookmarks on page 162.

2. Have students cut out and mount book marks onto construction paper using white glue.

3. Have students use hole punch to create hole in end of bookmark as indicated by dot. Students may then write any message they wish on their bookmarks.

4. Show students how to fold a 10" piece of ribbon in half so that the ends meet, and then how to thread the looped end of ribbon through the hole in the bookmark, threading the raw ends of ribbon through the loop and then pulling tight.

OTHER

Possibilities for Your Students

- Make Book Markers in various shapes.
- Make a Book Marker from a photograph. Glue a composition on to the back of their photo.

Cassette Tapes

Materials:

- cassette tapes • tape recorder • bell • student compositions

Directions:

1. Tell students: you will need to practice reading your composition to your partner. If you have something like a story or advertisement, you can divide it up so that each of you can read a part.

2. Next, you and your partner will read your composition slowly and clearly into a cassette tape recorder. You may want to add sound effects.

3. If you have a book that you've created, after you read each page, your partner will ring this bell so people listening to your story will know when to look at a new page as they follow along in your book.

Certificates

Materials:

• copies of the certificates on page 166 • glue • markers • glitter • gold seals, foil stars or sparkle stickers • paper ribbon

Directions:

1. Make copies of the certificate on page 166 available to the class.

2. Have students write out detailed reasons for the award including the name(s) of the recipient(s).

3. Invite students to decorate certificates with markers, glued-on glitter, foil stars, sparkle stickers or ribbons.

4. Students may then present completed certificates to each other (as recognition for friendly deeds) , to family members, to school personnel and to community helpers (in recognition for the helpful work they do), etc. Certificates may also be presented as "Thank You" notes to people who participate in your class program, or to people in the community whom you have visited during field trips, etc.

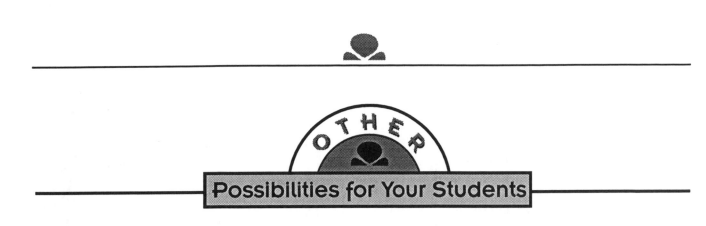

Possibilities for Your Students

- Instead of presenting the certificate flat have students roll it up and tie it with colorful yarn or ribbon. The certificate paper rolls up better if it has not been attached to construction paper.

- Instead of purchasing gold seals have your students make their own seals. One way to make a seal is to cut it out of colorful contact paper. This works will because the contact paper is self sticking. A circle or circular shape plus tails is easiest for students to cut our. Students with good fine motor skills can make a more complicated starburst shape.

  Another method creates a seal with a colorful ribbon. First cut out a wallpaper circle about 2" in diameter. Also cut a six or seven inch piece of ribbon. Cut a notch out of each end of the ribbon, then fold in half. Place the folded ribbon under the circle and staple them together. Now staple both to the certificate.

Certificate
of
Achievement

Signature

Class Newspaper

Materials:

• copy paper • copy machine

Directions:

1. Have students brainstorm to come up with a title for their class newspaper.

2. Have students work together to transfer the title and a class newspaper logo of their own design to the top of the paper.

3. Make copies of the newspaper. Then, after dating your edition, and after jotting in any teacher-messages, glue student-generated news, stories and illustrations to the blank space below the title. Use more than one page, if necessary. Make enough copies of the newspaper for each child to take one home.

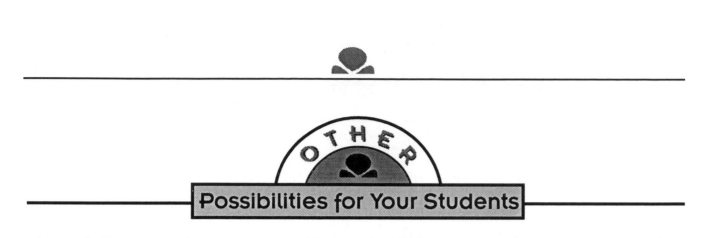

Possibilities for Your Students

- Instead of just requesting students to submit news, ask them to write: front page stories with large leadlines, "local" or class news, editorials, recipes, safety tips, advice columns, how-to columns, comic strips, advertisements, classified ads, crossword puzzles, sports articles, etc.

- For further information about starting your own newspaper read the article "What's New in Class Newspapers?", Instructor, May 1984.

Dice

Materials:

typing paper • pencil • scissors • tape

Directions:

1. Label one die by writing nouns in each of the 6 squares which have a dot in the center.

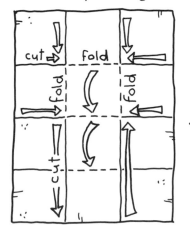

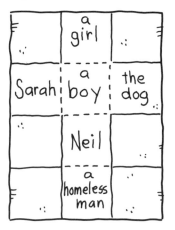

2. Fold on all of the dotted lines and crease each fold with your fingernail.

3. Cut on the straight lines.

4. Fold in the sides of the die and crease the folds.

5. Make sure all six of your words/phrases show. If one is hiding, change how you have folded the die.

6. Once you have all the words showing, tape this die together.

7. Repeat on the other three dice. One die should be all adjectives. Another should be all past-tense verbs. And the last die should be adverbs.

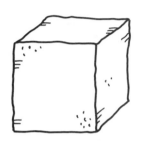

9. Roll the dice. Read the dice and then make the words into a sentence. For example if your rolled the words "carefully", "Sarah", shouted","funny" and "tired", your could make the sentence "The funny but tired Sarah shouted carefully at her dog." You earn one point for each word that you put into the sentence.

Possibilities for Your Students

• Instead of using the light weight typing paper, use construction paper for each different die. Or use a different colored marker for each of the die.

• Put students to work in cooperative groups of four, five, or six students. Assign each student only one type of die- nouns, verbs, adverbs, or adjectives to make. When a student plays in these larger groups, there are a lot of dice to roll. This can be managed by having each student in the game roll one die for the person who is the current player.

• Make dice as gifts for younger students in 1st or 2nd grades.

- If your students might find the cutting and folding too difficult, use a simpler die pattern. Cut this pattern out of tag board or light weight cardboard such as comes on twelve-pack soft drinks.

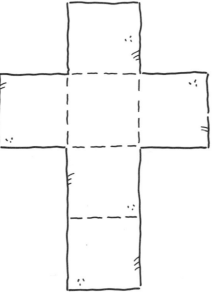

- Tape each die together. Have the students write the words on slips of paper and glue these on to the dice.

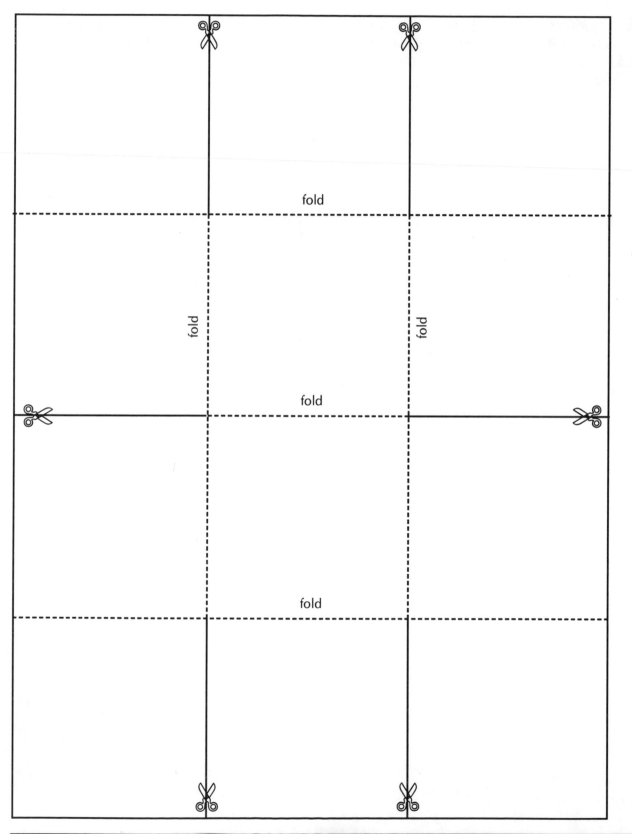

fold

fold

fold

fold

fold

Flip 'em Charts

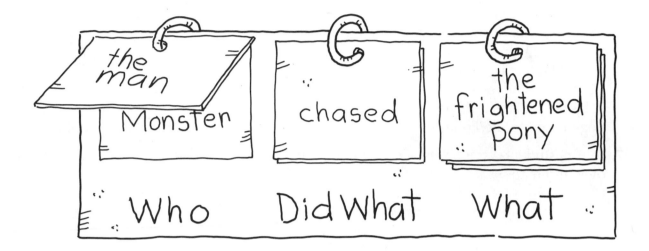

Materials:

• corrugated cardboard cut to 8″ x 24″ rectangles • index cards 4″ x 6″ • three large metal loose leaf rings • fine-line marker • glue • hole punch

Directions:

Invite students to:

1. Hold one index card horizontally and fold in half to create vertical fold in center of card.

2. Open card up and punch hole in fold approximately 1/2″ down from top of card. Use this card to guide holes punched in the rest of the cards so the cards will be uniform.

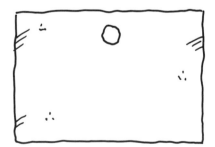

3. Lay cardboard down and arrange three of the prepared index cards next to each other approximately 1/2″ from top of cardboard. Use a pencil to indicate where the three holes punched in the index cards appear over the cardboard.

4. Remove cards and poke holes in cardboard where indicated.

5. Insert rings through holes in cardboard; lock in place.

6. Label chart so that students can make stacks of cards representing three sets of criteria such as:
Who / Did What/ Where
Who /Did What/ When
Noun/Verb/ Adverb
Subject/Predicate/Object
Beginning/Middle/Ending

7. To use, students attach sets of cards to rings and flip any combination of the three cards over and read.

OTHER
Possibilities for Your Students

• Make corrugated portion of chart large enough (16″ x 24″) to accommodate three sequence pictures taped below index cards. Students may then write sets of caption cards to accompany each of the illustrations.

Jugs

If I were the principal I would...

Materials:

- plastic jug (laundry soap, bleach, milk) • matte knife • permanent markers • cardboard
- paper fasteners • scissors

Directions:

1. (Prior to the activity make sure the jugs have been carefully rinsed and have been aired out. Otherwise the residual odor may cause students' eyes to become irritated.).

2. Invite students to: Use a permanent marker and a ruler to draw a 3 1/2" wide by 1" deep slot across the back of the jug. Or cut out the slot pattern and trace around it.

3. Next cut out the slot. Work slowly. It is easy to make the slot too large.

4. To keep the jug from rolling, cut two large feet out of the leftover cardboard.

5. Use the pointed end of your scissors to punch a small hole in the heel of each foot. Push a paper fastener through the hole of each foot.

6. Since jugs vary so much in shape you will need to estimate where the feet should be placed on your jug. Mark these two points with the permanent marker. Use your scissors to carefully punch two holes in the jug.

7. Now attach each foot to the underside of the jug with the large paper fasteners. You will need to put one hand through the slot to fasten the brad.

8. Test your jug to see if it will stand without rolling. If it rolls, remove one foot, and punch a new hole. Reassemble and test again. If the jug stands without rolling, go on to the next direction.

9. Now decide how to decorate your jug. Use permanent markers, contact paper, felt, pipe cleaners, etc.

10. Cut out a T-shaped pattern. Thoughtfully plan how you can cut 10 T-shaped patterns out of your cardboard. Lay this pattern on some cardboard and trace around it.

11. Cut out all 10 T-shaped patterns. Write one question that you have composed at the top (crossbar) of the T-shaped card. Write its answer at the bottom of the T-shaped card.

12. Stack the cards and place them in the slot in your Jug. To use the Jug have a friend read a question on the first T and answer it. Then your friend should unscrew the cap of the jug and peek inside to check the answer.

13. If the answer is correct, pull it out and lay the T-shaped card aside. If the answer is wrong, pull out the T-shaped card out and reinsert it in the slot in the jug after all the other cards.

OTHER Possibilities for Your Students

- Coat the jug with papier maché. Mix three cups of water and one and one half cup flour. Heat until the paste becomes thick. Tear long but narrow strips of newspaper. Dip strips of newspaper into the paste until they are coated. Drape the newspaper strips around the jug until it is covered. Let the jug dry overnight before painting it.

- Encourage students to use their imagination to create different styles of jugs. Twenty ounce and larger plastic pop bottles can also be made into jugs. If students use a different type of jug, change the T pattern to fit.

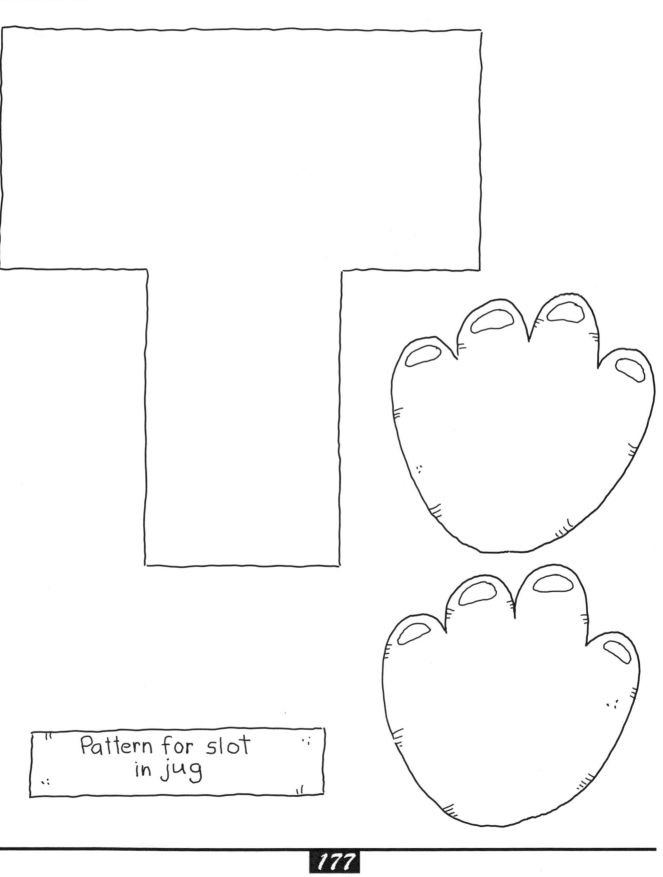

Pattern for slot
in jug

Neck Tags

Materials:

• copies of neck tags on page 180 • scissors • yarn pieces cut to 16" • construction paper (optional) • glue • markers • hole punch

Directions:

1. Offer students copies of the neck tags on page 180.

2. Have students use glue to mount the page onto construction paper (optional). Let dry.

3. Have students use scissors to cut neck tags apart.

4. Help students use hole punch to make holes at spots indicated

5. Assist students who need help in tying ends of yarn through holes.

6. Invite students to use neck tags to log stories (or poems, or character sketches, or personal statements, etc.) for each other to read.

Possibilities for Your Students

- Have students use name tags to list a series of facts about a person, place or thing, followed by a question such as, "Who am I?" or "What am I?" Use the other side of neck tag to record the answer to the riddle.

- If you want the Neck Tags to last longer than a few days, collect them and have them laminated before direction two.

- Make Neck Tags of various shapes and sizes.

- Make two Neck Tags and put them both on one piece of yarn. Wear one Neck Tag hanging on your front and one on your back.

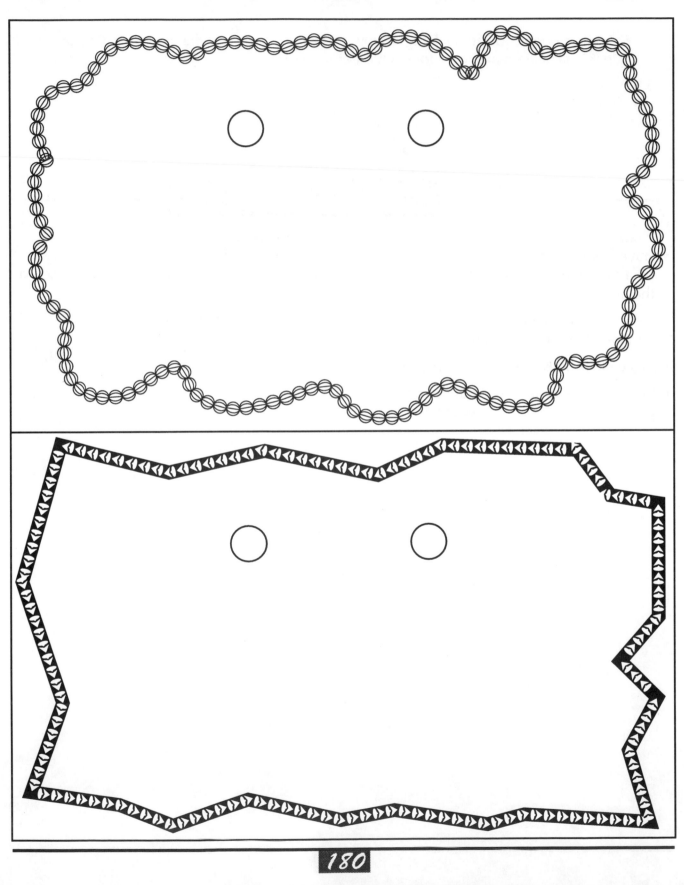

Pencil Riders

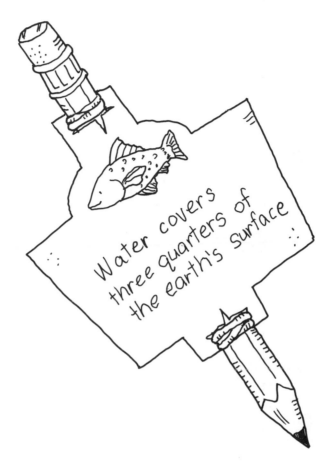

Water covers three quarters of the earth's surface

≡ Materials:

• copies of the pattern on page 182 • glue • construction paper • scissors • pencils and markers • rubber bands

≡ Directions:

1. Have students use white glue to mount pattern page on construction paper.

2. Let dry and have students cut out.

3. Help students cut x marks on riders open. Then, invite students to write special messages on each rider.

4. Have students slip riders over pencils and then wind rubber bands around pencils at each rider base to hold rider in place.

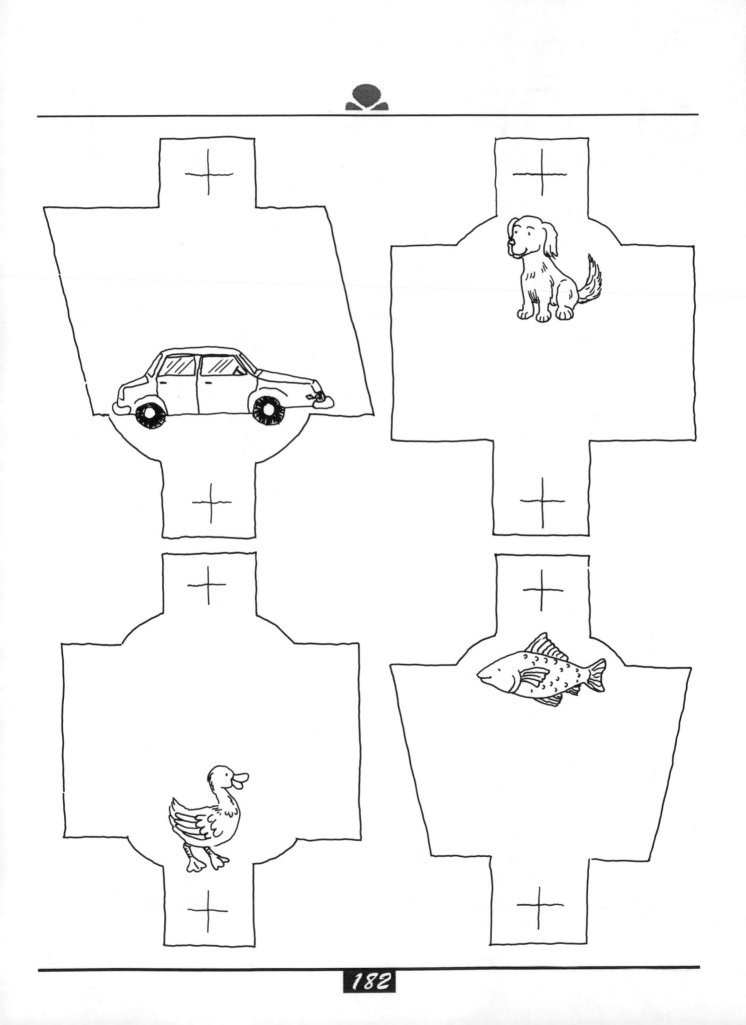

Pop a Balloon

Materials:

• notebook paper • 8" to 10" balloon of medium to heavy thickness • ball point pen (medium point works the best) • plastic twist-ties

Directions:

1. (Before doing this activity, find a business in your area which will give you 35 or more balloons. Speak to the owner or manager of local restaurants, fast food places, banks, lumber companies etc. Also guide students through the writing process so that they will have something to put into their balloon.)

2. Blow up your balloon.

3. Twist the neck of the balloon then fasten it with a twist tie to keep the balloon full of air.

4. Find a spot on the balloon that is empty. Use a ball point pen (medium point) to write "Pop this balloon with a pin to find a message." Write slowly and carefully. Don't press hard or else you'll pop the balloon. Let the ink dry so it won't smear.

5. Unfasten the twist tie to let the air come out.

6. Write your composition on a half sheet of note paper. Your paper must be small or it won't fit into the balloon.

7. Fold your paper in half and then in half again.

8. Fold your paper in half one more time, then roll it up.

9. Slide the rolled paper into the balloon. If the paper gets stuck pull it out and roll it more tightly.

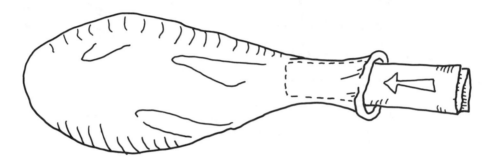

10. Blow your balloon up and tie a knot before you give it to someone.

OTHER
Possibilities for Your Students

• Fill the balloons with helium instead of air. Allow students to let the balloons go outside.

Portfolios

≡ Materials:

- construction paper or wallpaper, pre-cut to 18″ x 24″ • ruler • pencil • scissors
- stapler

≡ Directions:

Invite students to:

1. Fold your paper in half so that it becomes 18″ by 12″. Crease the fold with your fingernail. Then open your paper.

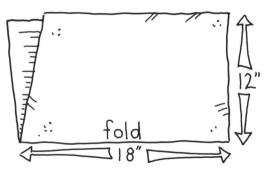

2. Along the shorter (18″) edge measure 1/2″ in from the edge of the paper and mark the spot with a pencil. Do this five times at different spots along the edge.

3. Using your ruler, connect these marks in a straight line. Then repeat along the other (opposite) 18″ edge.

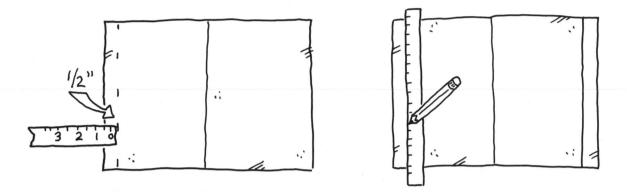

4. Next on the longer edge measure 5″ up from the bottom of the paper and mark it. Repeat until you have 5 or 6 marks to help you.

5. Using your ruler and these dots, draw straight line across the bottom of your future portfolio.

6. Starting at the top of your portfolio, cut on the half inch line until you reach the fold. Discard this long thin piece. Repeat on the other side of your portfolio.

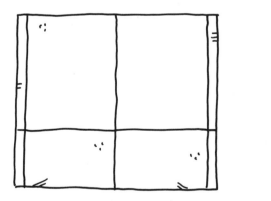
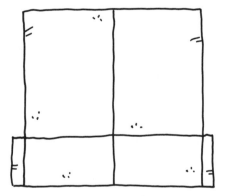

7. Bend in each flap on the line.

8. Carefully fold up the bottom of your portfolio on the 5 inch line. Crease the fold with your fingernail.

9. Notice where the flap touches the back of your folder. Spread glue on this part of each flap. Be careful to use only a little glue.

10. Press down so that each flap attaches to the inside of your portfolio.

11. Lay your portfolio aside to dry before you use it to store your compositions.

- Laminate the construction paper to make it more durable.

- A much simpler portfolio can be made without flaps by using a stapler instead. Skip steps 3, 4, 5, 10, 11, 12, 13, 14. These portfolios do not hold as much.

- If you plan for students to file many compositions in their portfolios, after Step 8 have students draw a second line at the 6 inch level. They should end up with two straight lines about 1 inch apart. At this time students should crease the 6 inch line.

- Another way to increase the amount one portfolio will hold is to draw a line down either side of the center fold. These lines should be drawn 1/2 inch on either side of the center fold. Fold and then crease each of these lines separately.

- A portfolio with one side pocket instead of bottom pockets can be made from 18" x 24" paper. First cut off a 5 inch strip so that you create a 13" x 24" sheet. Measure in 4 inches from one of the shorter ends. Fold and crease on this line to create the pocket. Staple the left and right sides of the pocket. Now fold the portfolio in half and you are done.

Sack Puppets

Materials:

• small paper sacks • glue • white and colored construction paper or tag board • crayons or felt tipped markers • scissors

Directions:

1. Make copies of the blank puppet faces on pages 190 through 198. (Pass out several different puppet faces, jaw patterns, and extra facial parts.)

2. Draw and color your puppet's face.

3. Next glue your puppet's face to a piece of construction paper or tag board. This will make it stronger.

4. When the glue is dry, cut out your puppet's face and jaw parts.

5. Take one paper bag. Lift the fold and glue the puppet's jaw below the fold. It is important to glue the mouth piece on before you glue on the head so that the mouth will be properly aligned.

6. Glue the head to the bottom of the sack so that it is aligned with the jaw piece.

7. Choose a partner. Use your two puppets to act out the composition you and your partner wrote.

OTHER

Possibilities for Your Students

- Create a puppet stage by draping a sheet over a long table or several student desks. Create a scene on some butcher paper and tape it to a wall or a large bookcase or doorway.

- Cut puppet eyes, noses, ears, mouths, and arms out of construction paper or magazines. Or glue on buttons for eyes, yarn for hair, hats, glasses, beards.

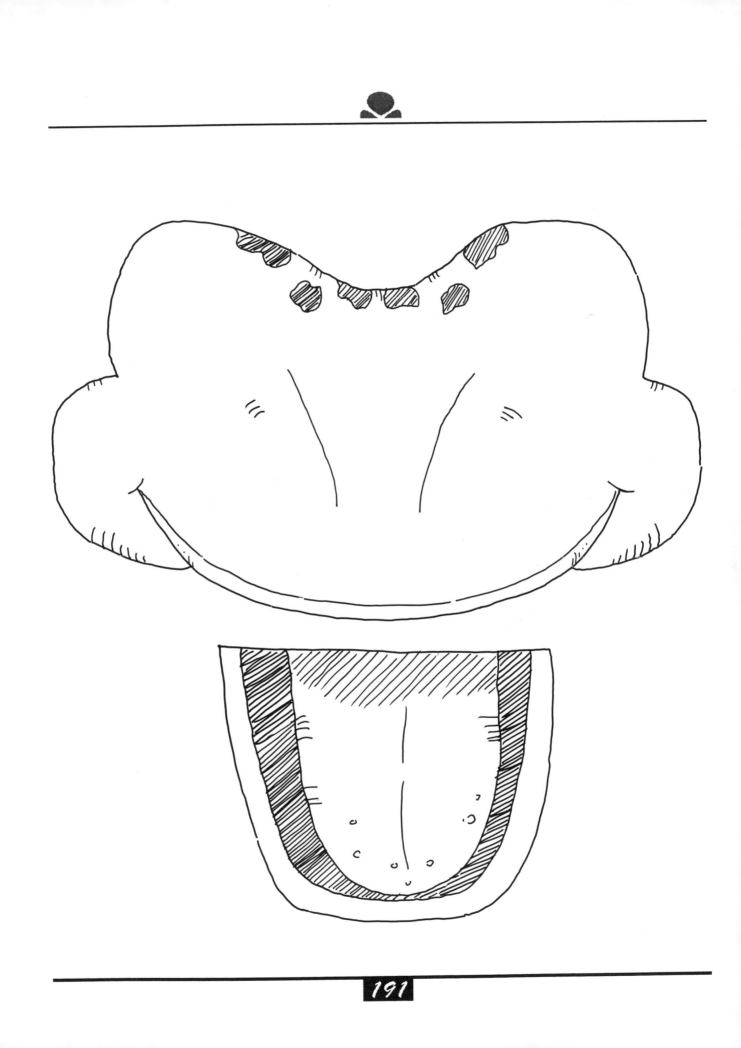

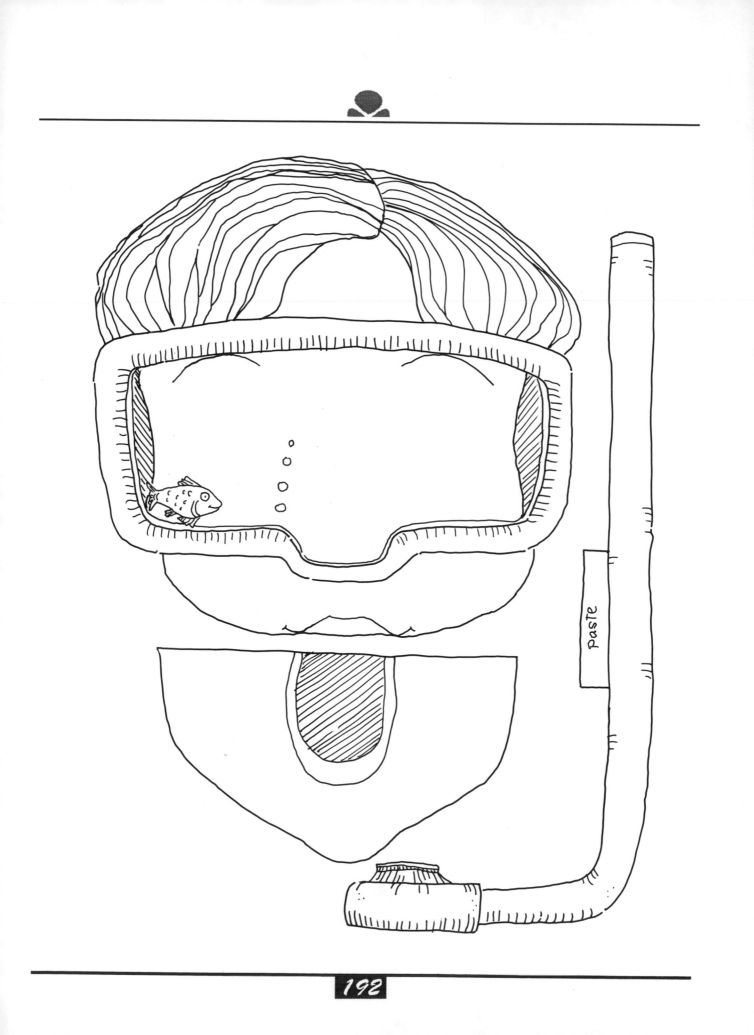

paste

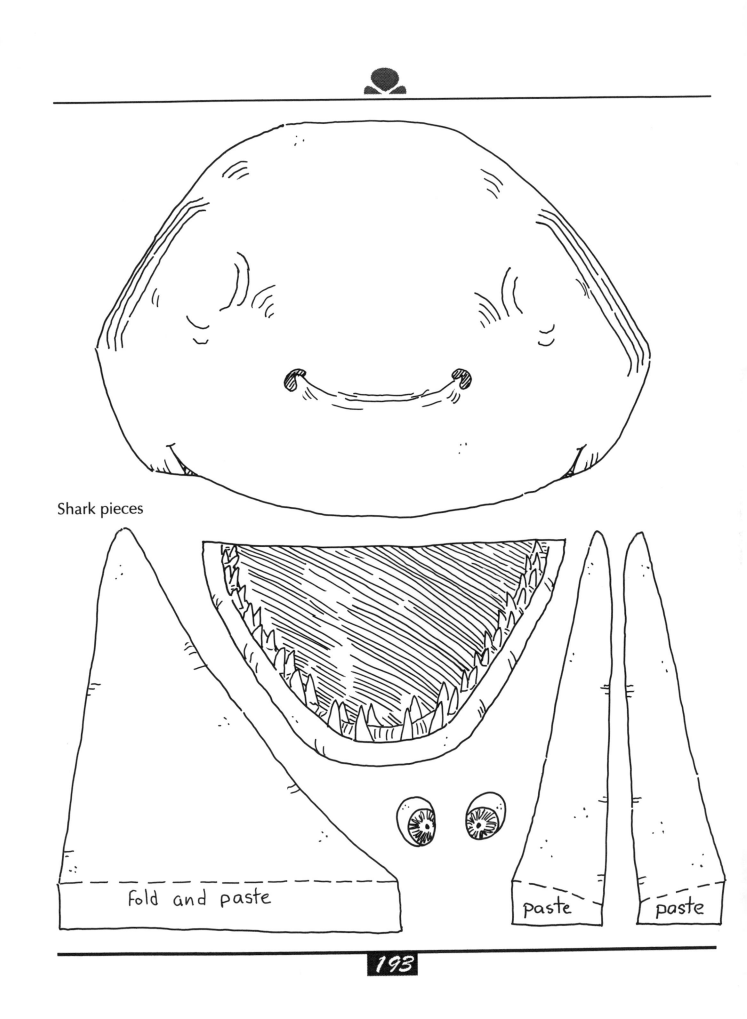

Shark pieces

fold and paste

paste

paste

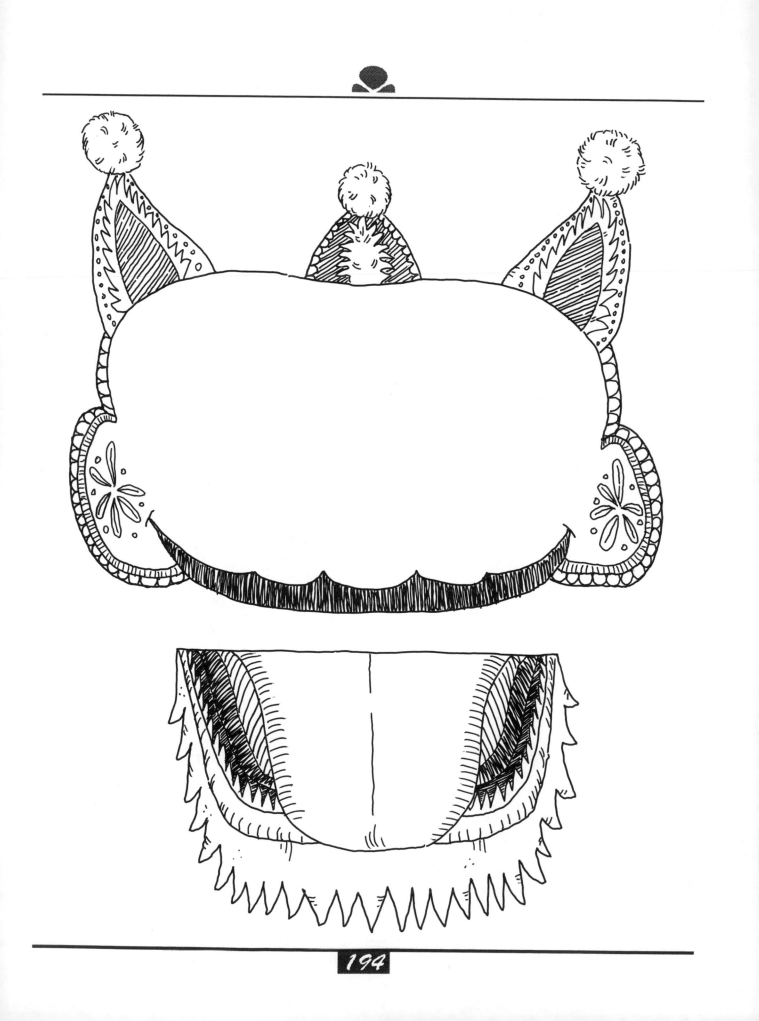

Frog pieces

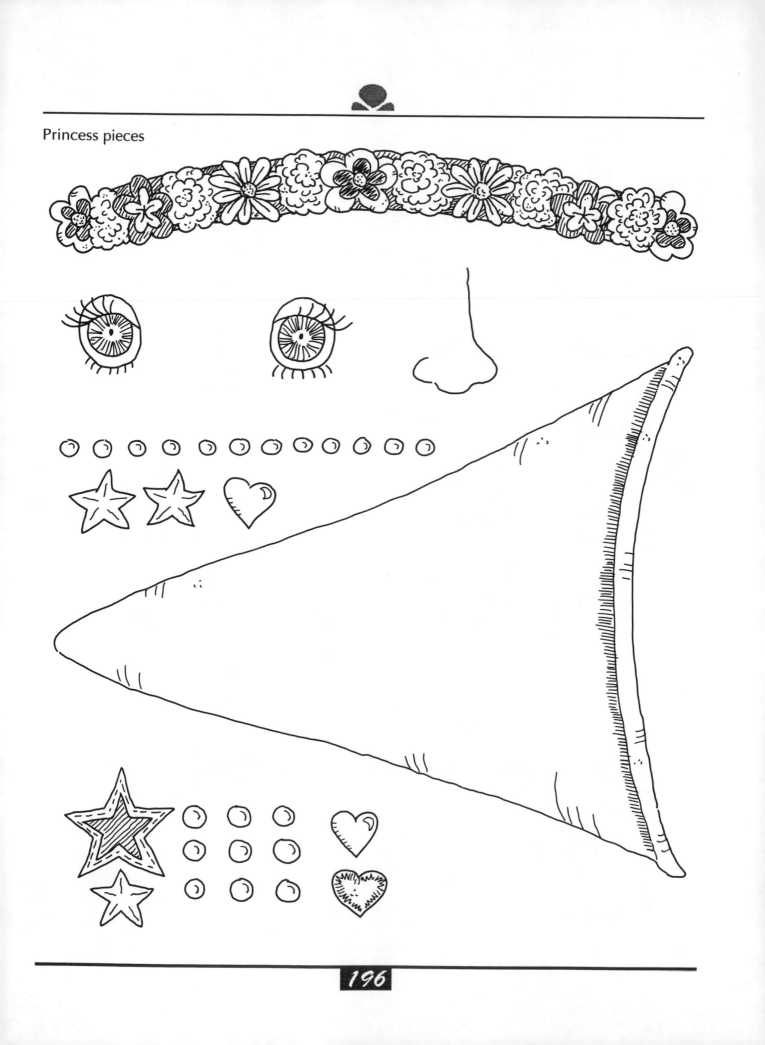

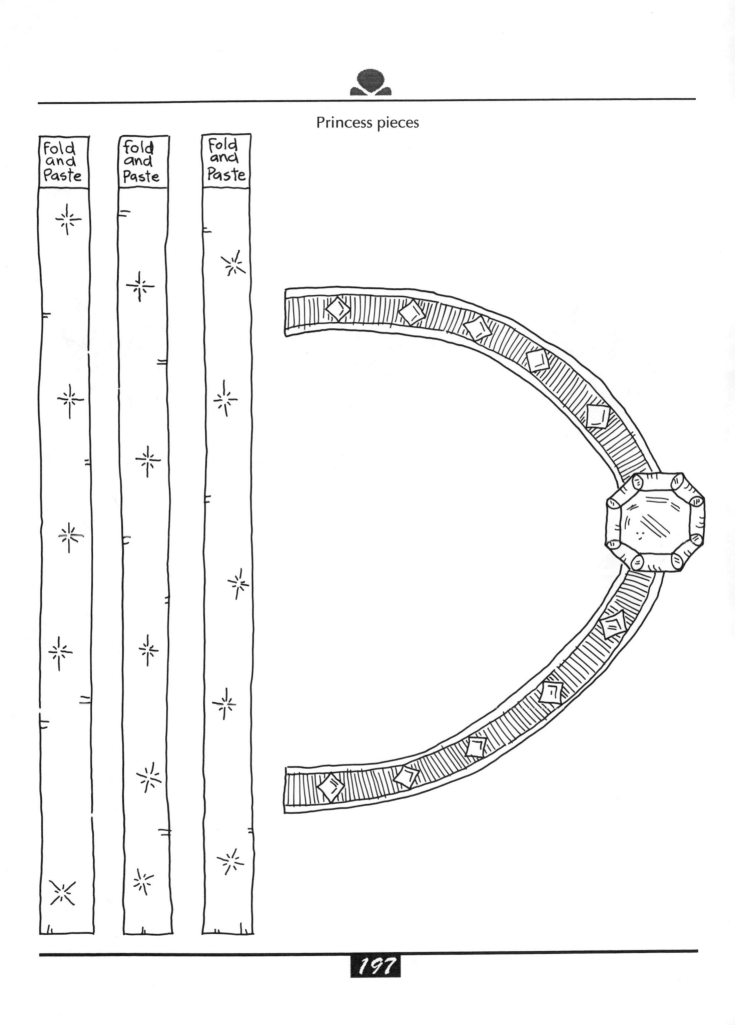

Chinese dragon pieces

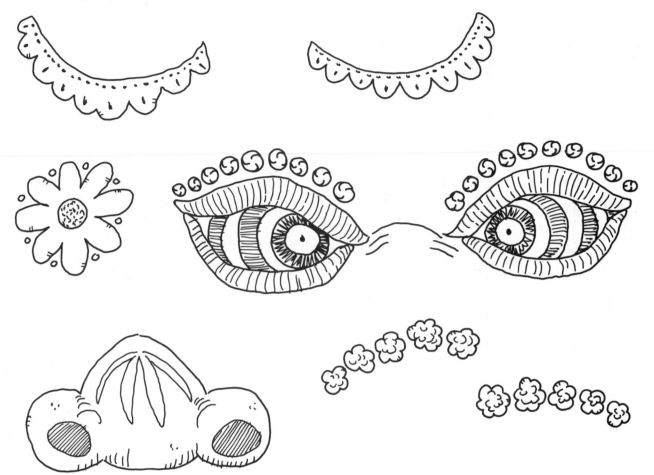

Scuba diver pieces

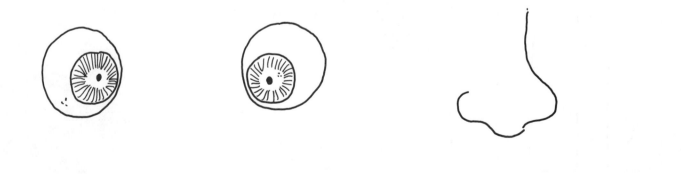

Sliders

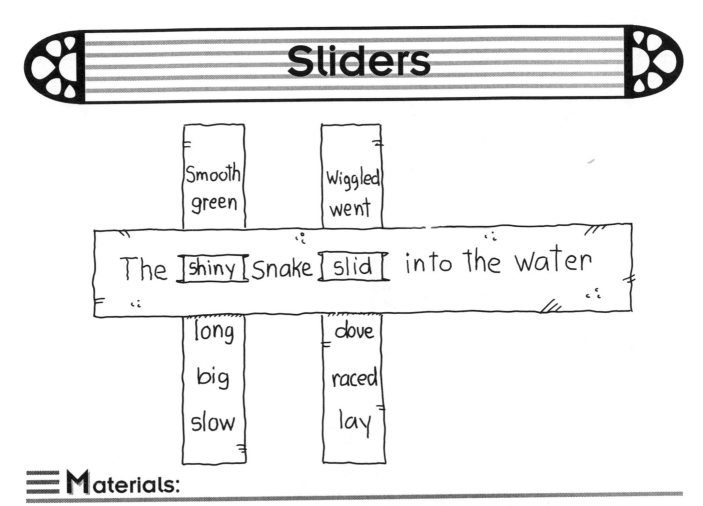

Smooth green

Wiggled went

The [shiny] [Snake] [slid] into the water

long big slow

dove raced lay

Materials:

- copies of slider strips on page 201 • glue • oaktag cut into pieces 5" x 18" pieces
- markers • craft knife (teacher use only)

Directions:

1. Have students use glue to mount slider strips onto construction paper. Let dry and have students cut strips apart.

2. Use craft knife to cut open desired number of slits in sliders. (Width of slits needs to be slightly wider than that of sliders.)

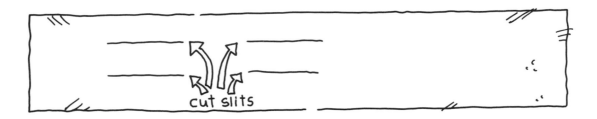

cut slits

3. Show students how to weave strips into slider. Then, offer students sentence possibilities to print on their sliders, such as:

* The_____snake_____into the water.

* The_____girl felt_____at her party.

* The_____pizza tasted_____.

* The _____boat_____on the water.

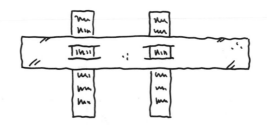

4. Have students fill in spaces on strips with a variety of silly or sensible word choices that, when slid into place, will complete the sentences.

OTHER
Possibilities for Your Students

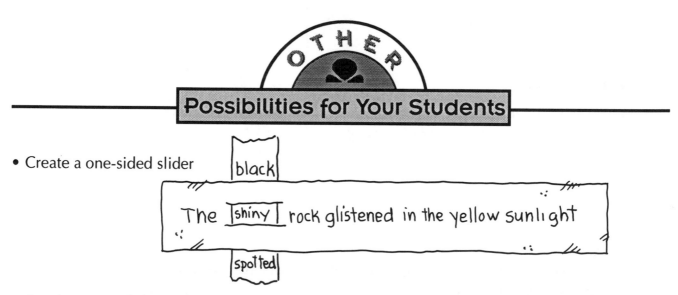

• Create a one-sided slider

black

The [shiny] rock glistened in the yellow sunlight

spotted

• Cut the strips of paper about two inches longer. After the words are written on each strip of paper, help the student staple the top of a particular strip to the bottom of that strip. This will keep the strips from falling out.

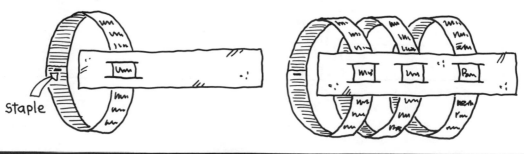

staple

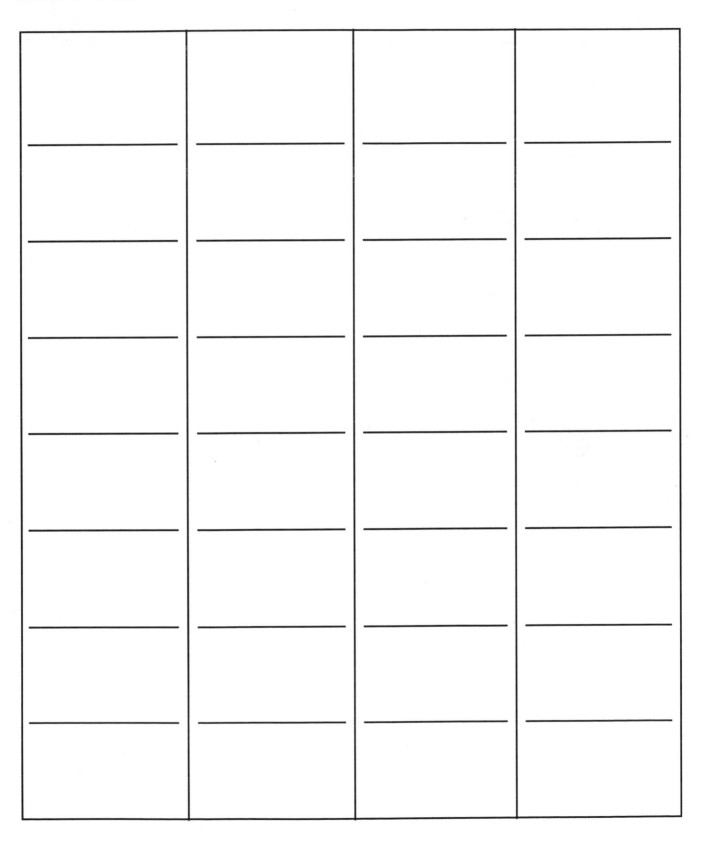

Spinners

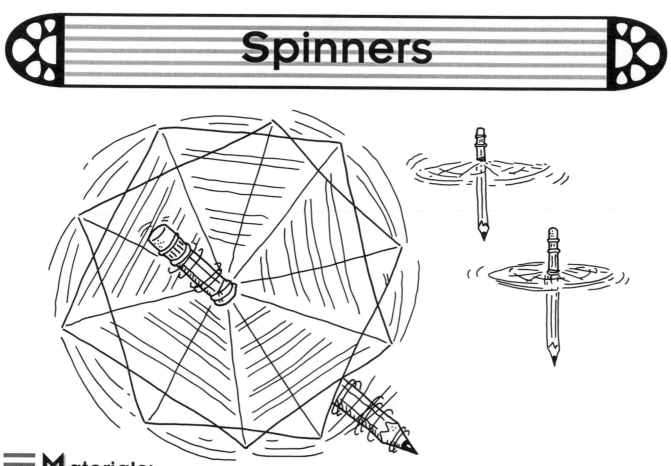

Materials:

• old file folders or light weight cardboard (empty flattened-out cereal boxes) • short pencil • rubberbands • scissors • glue

Directions:

1. Before class duplicate one copy of the pentagon pattern on page 204 for each student. Distribute and invite students to:

2. Use scissors to cut out the pentagon.

3. Write your information such as a weather forecast or a safety tip in one section of the spinner. Turn the spinner clockwise and write new information in the next section of the spinner. Continue turning the spinner clockwise until all your information has been written on the spinner.

4. Next glue the pentagon on to one half of a file folder (or other light weight cardboard) with rubber cement. If white glue is used, smooth out the pentagon and let dry before continuing.

5. Again cut out around your pentagon.

6. Punch a very tiny hole in the center of the pentagon with your scissors. Then stick a short pencil through the hole.

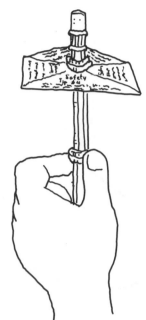

7. Wrap a rubberband around the pencil several times until it is snug. Then work the rubberband up or down the pencil until it is next to the pentagon. Repeat this at the other end of the pencil. The rubberband will keep the pentagon from slipping off the pencil. Adjust the spinner so that it is in the middle of the pencil.

8. Take turns using the spinner The person who spins is the one who receives the information. His/her information is the one that faces the ground.

Possibilities for Your Students

• Instead of having the pencil lead touch the ground reverse things so that the eraser touches the ground. Or make a five sided spinner, six, or eight sided spinner.

• Write a question on the top side of the spinner and the answer on the other side directly below the question.

• Make a different kind of spinner from a paper plate, a brad, and a pointer.

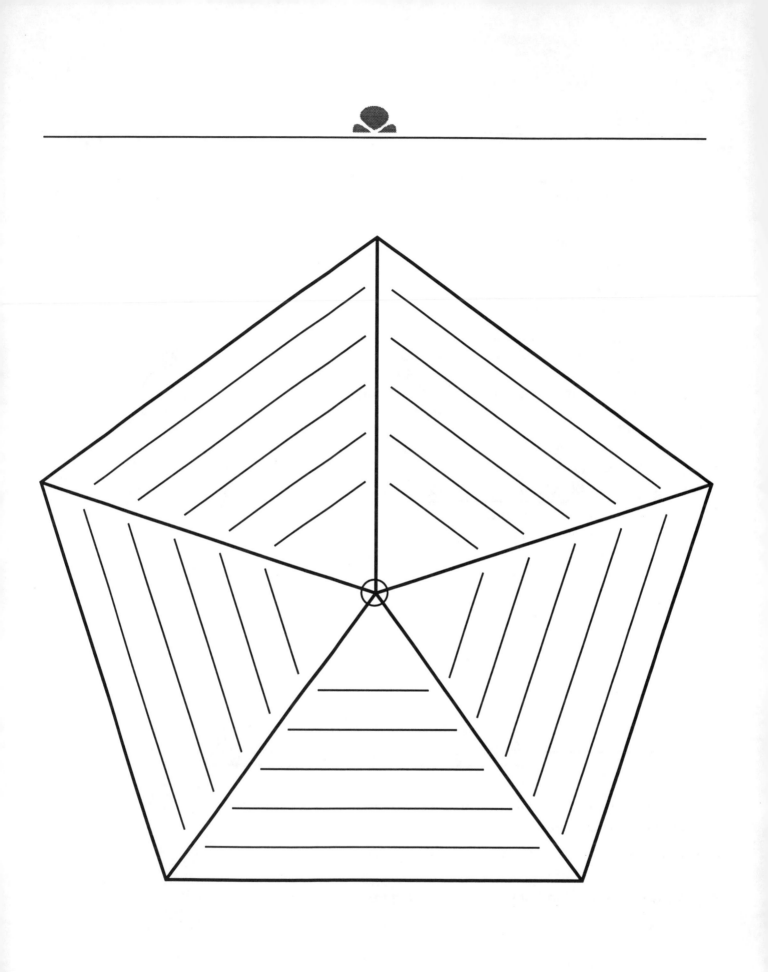

Tags and Tickets

Materials:

• copies of the tag and ticket patterns found on pages 207 and 208 • scissors • yarn or string • hole punch • markers • clear, self-adhesive paper

Directions:

1. Have students use glue to mount tickets and tags onto construction paper. Let dry and have students cut apart

2. Punch hole in top of each tag and thread yarn or string through hole.

3. Have students use tags to label items in the room, or for pricing items at a pretend store center.

4. Have students write information on tickets allowing ticket holder admission to a specific classroom event, or promising ticket holder "one good deed," etc.

Possibilities for Your Students

• Instead of using hole reinforcers, put two pieces of tape on the part of the tag that will have the hole. Punch the hole through the tape. The remaining tape will strengthen the paper around the hole and help keep it from tearing.

• Instead of using the tag pattern, have students make the tags in the form of large shapes.

• Instead of using yarn or string, use elastic thread. Students like the elastic because it will stretch to fit around many objects and/or body parts. This can be purchased at a fabric store.

• Tags can also be made by folding a rectangular piece of paper.

1. Fold in the right and left so that they meet in the center.

2. Then fold enough of the tip back that you have room to punch a hole.

Ticket

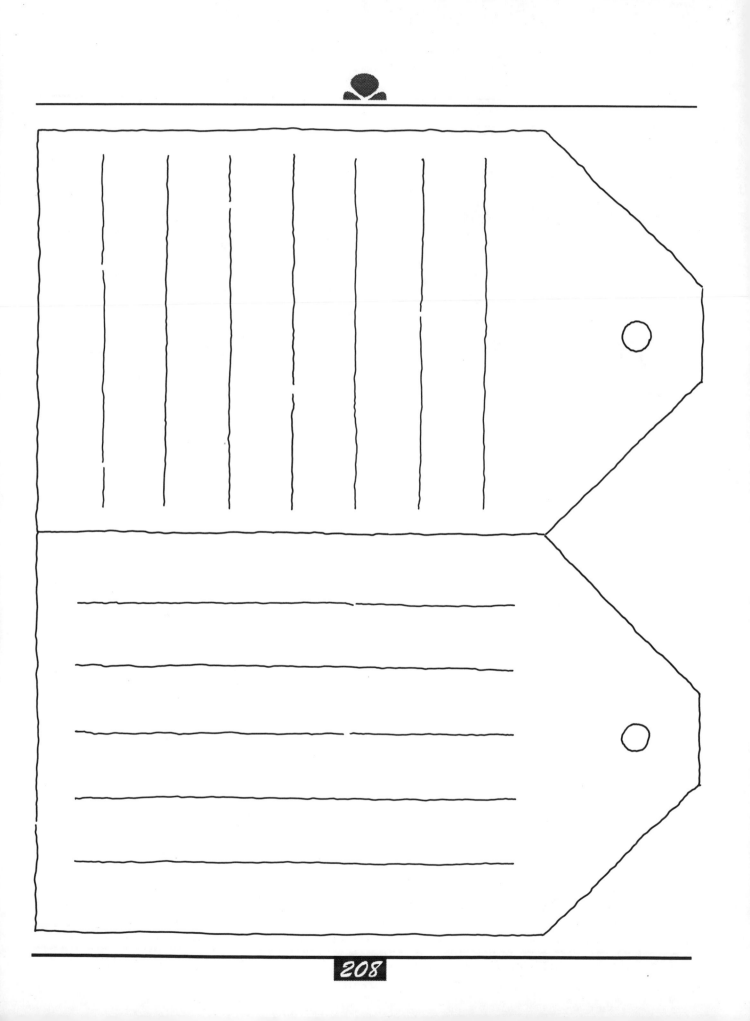